D0983985

Inventing **Black-on-Black** Violence

Space, Place, and Society
John Rennie Short, *Series Editor*

INVENTING
BLACK·ON·BLACK
VIOLENCE

discourse, space, and representation

DAVID WILSON

SYRACUSE UNIVERSITY PRESS

Copyright © 2005 by Syracuse University Press
Syracuse, New York 13244-5160

All Rights Reserved

First Edition 2005

05 06 07 08 09 10   6 5 4 3 2 1

The paper used in this publication meets the minimum requirements of American
National Standard for Information Sciences—Permanence of Paper for Printed
Library Materials, ANSI Z39.48-1984∞™

Library of Congress Cataloging-in-Publication Data
Wilson, David, 1956–
    Inventing black-on-black violence : discourse, space, and representation /
David Wilson.—1st ed.
       p. cm—(space, place, and society)
    Includes bibliographical references and index.
    ISBN: 0-8156-3080-8 (hardcover : alk. paper)
  1. Crime and race—United States.   2. Violence—United States—Public opinion.
3. African American youth—Public opinion.   4. Inner cities—United States—
Public opinion.   5. Fear of crime—United States.   6. Crime in mass media.
7. African Americans in mass media.   8. Discourse analysis.   I. Title.   II. Series.
HV6789.W525   2005
364.3'496'073—dc22   2004028510

Manufactured in the United States of America

Contents

◢ ◢ ◢

Illustrations

Figure

Tables

David Wilson is an associate professor of geography at the University of Illinois at Urbana-Champaign. He has written *Derelict Landscapes: The Wasting of America's Built Environment* (with John Jakle). He has edited *Marginalized Places: A Structurationist Agenda* (with Jim Huff) and *The Urban Growth Machine: Critical Perspectives Two Decades Later* (with Andrew Jonas). His work has appeared in such journals as *Political Geography, Urban Geography, Annals of the American Academy of Social and Political Sciences, Space and Polity, Urban Affairs Quarterly, Professional Geographer,* and *Antipode.*

✒ ✒ ✒
Preface

In U.S. cities after 1980, violence involving African American perpetrators and victims increased (Tonry and Morris 1984; Page 1987). A
wealth of statistics, ethnographies, anecdotal accounts, and national reporting makes this increase difficult to refute. But such escalation is not
surprising. Plagued by massive loss of decent paying jobs, stigmatized
identities and residential settings, institutional withdrawal of resources,
and unabated physical decay, these participants in violence responded to
circumstances in destructive if predictable ways. Since recorded time,
oppressive living conditions have spawned hopelessness and violence; this
circumstance has been no exception. In this sense, nineteenth-century
Jews in Europe, twentieth-century Catholics in Belfast, twentieth-
century "Coloreds" in South Africa, and late-twentieth-century African
Americans in daunting ghettos have shared this bond (compare Fair and
Ostroff 1991; *Europe Traveled* 1991; and Herman, Jacobson, and Moffat
1997).

But many have made sense of this violence by blaming African
Americans: their ways, values, beliefs, and lifestyles—in short, their "culture." Like recent social processes in inner cities, discourses about this issue
placed a dominant societal notion of blackness at center stage. Image-rich
offerings of "black-on-black violence" interpreted through mainstream
understandings fingered a morally and culturally failing youth. Reports
invoked a luminous reality of "black inner cities," "roaming black youths
and gangs," "underclass subcultures," and "black families" to understand
this violence. Black kids, black men and women, black families, and black
politicians were caricatured, placed in horrifically declining settings that
reinforced public stereotypes of black youth and their communities. In

ix

this context, any meaningful role played by society, economy, and structure was communicatively marginalized.

This book explores the construction of this violence vision. Employing a constructionist perspective sensitized to political economy, it chronicles how prominent mainstream sources, both conservative and liberal, created this issue and how it gained credibility in popular thought. Conservatives and liberals were authoritative and esteemed voices in American politics and worked aggressively to construct their renditions of this violence after 1980. These "schools," as before, offered subjective political realities, all the while claiming that they spoke core, uncompromising truths. These purportedly different but equally prominent sources offered conflicting interpretations of this violence, each virulently debating the other. But at a fundamental level their discourses were substantially similar, and together they created a common mainstream vision of "black-on-black violence." This book thus uncovers a different reality. By examining the process by which the concept of "black-on-black violence" was constructed and presented to the public, it delineates a new vision of this.

Social constructionism is an important way to understand social issues like this violence. It highlights the fundamental act of humans representing the world to create renditions of people, places, and processes (see Delgado and Stefancic 2001; Boghassian 2001). Understandings of the world are tied to human acts of representing more than an essential character of a reality "speaking directly" to us. In our case, a seemingly straightforward social issue—blunt acts of aggression upon human beings—becomes a contested site by those who wish to control how the issue is thought about and acted upon by people, institutions, and society. One facet of social constructionism, discourse analysis, recognizes coherent clusters of representations from unities of communicative forms (that is, from mixes of discussions, written texts, and pronouncements) that make different versions of this process. Such discourses simultaneously offer realities and seek to refute others.

The book's structure reflects my goals and line of thinking. Chapter 1 sets the stage for the empirical chapters by discussing the nature of discourse. Using the fundamental interrogative tool of spatiality, which offers human-made space as a key building ingredient of discourse, it explores how discourse can be identified and critically examined. Chapter 2 provides a foundation for the investigation of the conservative and liberal discourses by revealing the historical context for their emergence. It chronicles the prominent postwar forces and processes that created an evolving but consistently negative construction of inner city black youth and communities. Chapters 3 and 4, the core empirical chapters, discuss how the conservative and liberal discourses were constructed. They focus on these discourses' "fields of understanding"—that is, their staged comprehensions about cities, inner cities, African American youth, inner city institutions, and urban politicians, comprehensions that imperceptibly but powerfully framed discussions of this violence.

Chapter 5 compares the two discourses, exploring in detail why a prominent post-1980 discourse on black-on-black violence, presented with elaborate detail and embellishment, coalesced around the notion of underclass culture. It looks beyond the presentation of these discourses to see why this idea of an underclass culture resonated with mainstream America, bringing to light other communicative processes at work in the discourses that underscored their power and influence: their theatrical style of presentation and the image-laden concepts they used to speak their truths. Chapter 6 examines what I deem to be the most significant consequence of the post-1980 vision of black-on-black violence: its use as an explanation for the crime panic that swept across America after 1980. Drawing on contemporary sources, it documents the way in which politicians and the media used this vision to finger inner city blacks as the source of rising crime and to assign blame. Chapter 7, the conclusion, discusses the significance of this study's findings.

This book has a long and semisordid history that goes back to my days living in Indianapolis in the 1980s. My interviews of social and political leaders in that city at that time formed the starting point for this study. So many friends and colleagues helped this project that I must thank just a few. I owe an intellectual debt to the transnational group at the University of Illinois and the leadership of Jan Pieterse. Their energy and ideas lie embedded in this manuscript and continue to stimulate and challenge me. The Painkillers Blues Band and my 1974 Fender Stratocaster were constant sources of replenishment and sustenance. David Adcock, Steve Errede, David Hertzog, Carolyn Johnson, and Ryan Woodson play the blues like no one else. Finally, the endless hours of basketball in the front yard with Matty and Andy, with Mary Anne's support, kept this project afloat. My game never got much better, but the sheer exhilaration of so being in their lives sustained me. Without Matty, Andy, and Mary Anne, this book would have been impossible to complete, and I dedicate it to them.

Author's Note

I have used an analysis of interviews, media coverage, and the publications and pronouncements offered by pundits to look critically at the social construction of "black crime." Data acquisition to analyze the discourses was multistaged. First, I conducted open-ended interviews with city officials, local politicians, and organizational heads in Indianapolis and Chicago between 1986 and 1995. I also later conducted interviews with officials and politicians in St. Louis between 1998 and 2000 to add depth to this data. It is at this "ground level" of everyday political activity, according to Peter Goodrich (1987), that discourses on social issues are organized and widely communicated. In this important facet of discourse, ideas circulate through the everyday in debates, planning agendas, policy discussion, and informal social engagement. Thus, I interviewed mayoral candidates, city-county councilors, task force representatives, and social service heads about views on black-on-black violence and race. We discussed perceptions of this violence's intensity, causes, culprits, impacts on communities, and possible ameliorative measures. Respondents tended to be talkative and open about this issue. To ensure sound data, all respondents were provided the opportunity to be accorded a pseudonym if they preferred. Many respondents opted for this preference.

Next I conducted a content analysis of prominent urban newspapers in eight cities between 1980 and 1998: New York, Cleveland, Indianapolis, St. Louis, San Francisco, Chicago, Philadelphia, and Detroit. I studied prominent local dailies such as the *Chicago Sun-Times, Chicago Tribune, Cleveland Plain Dealer, St. Louis Post-Dispatch, and San Francisco Chronicle*, and community weeklies, such as the *Cleveland Call & Post, Los Angeles Sentinel, Chicago Defender, and Michigan Chronicle*. To be reviewed, articles had to contain the phrase "black violence" or "black-on-black violence." The articles were diverse in type and purpose, ranging from editorials and stories of community change to reports on specific incidents of violence and exposés of changing downtowns. The text, immensely rich, narrated the people, institutions, places, and processes supposedly involved in black-on-black violence as well as this process itself.

I also used two other data sources: a content analysis of magazines and of the *Rush Limbaugh Show*. In studying regional and national magazines, I searched through the *Reader's Guide to Periodical Literature* and the Web using the key phrases "black violence" and "black-on-black violence." It yielded articles from a cross-section of magazines, including *Time, Newsweek, U.S. News and World Report, Harpers, New Republic, Commentary,* and *Life*. These articles also frequently provided rich accounts of this issue as an emerging national trend. Black-on-black violence was on the public agenda and reportage was widespread. Analysis of the *Rush Limbaugh Show* between 1990 and 1999 was equally helpful; no text better captured the pulse of conservative thought in the 1990s. In streams of unadulterated diatribe, Limbaugh spoke deeply felt conservative beliefs in detail. Buffoonery aside, his ideas reflected the emergence in the 1980s of the new conservatism. All pieces offering direct statements about, and contextual setups for, black-on-black violence were analyzed as text. These pieces were seen to have a "text" and "subtext," an overt pronouncement about a social issue and less flagrant assertions about people, processes, and places that provided context for direct pronouncement. This emphasis on statement and context follows much recent discourse and textual analysis of social issues (see Parisi and Holcomb 1994; Ruddick 1996a, 1996b). Where these elements were contained in sentences, I highlighted them and made them available as quotations. In this process, I was particularly sensitive to the use of mental maps (one kind of Lefebvre's spaces of representation) in text. Such spaces were frequently provided much treatment; when used as quotations, I have sought to distill them typically to three or four sentences.

PART ONE

◢ ◢ ◢

Setting the Stage

1

The Nature of Discourse

The Context and Study

On the afternoon of January 8, 1981, a young African American in Chicago's Cabrini Green Housing Project was killed by black youth. The man, Larry Potts, twenty-one, an aspiring musician, was struck in the back by shots fired through a first-floor window while he was performing. He was the ninth victim in the area in two months. Reports of these killings, dubbed Chicago's "winter wave of violence" in the local press (Casey and Hough 1981), quickly captured national attention. In this context, stories in the *New York Times, Los Angeles Times, Washington Post, Cleveland Plain Dealer,* and newspapers across the country ignited a spark that seared public thought. In the media a new city ill had purportedly emerged: "black-on-black violence." Statistics about this violence were suddenly featured prominently from coast to coast. For example, data from University of Chicago law professor Michael Tonry and Norvel Morris of the University of Maryland were discovered and underscored in op-ed pieces across the nation (Tonry and Morris 1984). Their findings:

• Homicide was the leading cause of death for black men and women between the ages of twenty-five and thirty-four; black men from twenty-five through forty-four years old were eleven times more likely to die as homicide victims than were white men in that same age bracket.

• Although one of every nine Americans was black, one of every two male murder victims was black—as was one of every two people arrested for murder.

• Blacks were two and one-half times more likely than whites to be victims of rape or robbery.

3

TABLE 1

**Proportion of Articles on Local Violence Using
the Term "Black-on-Black Violence" in Text**

Source	1978	1980	1982	1984	1986
San Francisco Chronicle	0	0	2 (4%)	12 (24%)	14 (28%)
Chicago Tribune	0	0	3 (6%)	14 (28%)	18 (36%)
Cleveland Call & Post	0	0	3 (6%)	30 (60%)	41 (82%)
St. Louis Post Dispatch	0	0	1 (2%)	9 (18%)	16 (32%)

Source: Based on a random sample of fifty articles selected for each year. Articles selected for review had to have the words *violence* or *crime* in their titles and focus on local affairs.

The concept of "black-on-black violence" had sporadically surfaced to this point. But in the early 1980s the issue exploded on the national scene, with many diverse narrativists providing accounts (see table 1). These accounts further racialized this violence, offering evocative stories of black assailants assaulting black victims. At the core of this violence, in renditions, was blackness rather than poverty, economics, or class. Instead of economic circumstance or social situatedness, race was the template applied to understand this violence. In media hyperbole, here was proof that inner city blacks had become dangerously distanced from civility. Many narrativists communicated this violence as one more marker of a failing and problem people who had become dangerously discordant and self-destructive.

"Black-on-black violence" thereafter became widely discussed in Congress, public schools, mayoral forums, churches, and presidential speeches. To explain this phenomenon, Pennsylvania Senator Arlen Specter spoke to constituents of skyrocketing child abuse and the breakdown of family life; Chicago Mayor Jane Byrne reported in a press conference the decline of youth values and attitudes in ghetto neighborhoods; Sgt. Patrick Hallihan of the Mt. Prospect, Illinois, police told reporters that kids were not getting moral instruction in homes, churches, and schools. A common thread ran through these articulations: this violence followed from deteriorated culture in inner cities. Its most horrific by-product, free-wheeling youth in imploding inner cities, were imagined as bodies propelled along irrational paths of violence and destruction (see Mercer 1997).

Yet "black violence" is no more a reality than "youth violence" or "Italian violence." As Mike Males (1997) notes, talk of black violence is the equivalent of talking about blond-haired violence, blue-eyed violence, or left-handed violence. Males objects to categorizing and illuminating such a process on the basis of people's physical properties. Like a growing number of social scientists, Males supports a social constructionist perspective to understand this issue. He identifies many possible ways this violence could have been constructed (see also Pulido 1998; Schein 1999, 2002). The way this violence came to be known, to Males, was from one scripted version that simultaneously offered one rendition and excluded others. I agree with Males: We must never lose sight of "black-on-black violence" as a construction that "led first" with mainstream imaginings of race. The mainstream could have deracialized, moderately racialized, or intensely racialized this issue; the latter was the case.

Not surprisingly, this constructing of urban violence did not go undetected by progressives in the early 1980s and beyond. Conservatives were widely proclaimed to choreograph this dominant take. They supposedly used African American stereotypes established over decades to offer crude renditions of freewheeling and routinely violent youth (Lusane 1993; Wacquant 1994a). In these starkly conservative times, to liberals and radicals, conservatives openly chronicled inner city blacks as angry and dangerously removed from normal life. Stereotype was perpetuated and conservatives were responsible. It is, of course, hard to dispute this conservative role. Many conservative commentators, think-tank moguls, reporters, and politicians deftly drew on and extended prevailing understandings of race, culture, citizenship, and space to implicate African American subcultures, families, institutions, and communities (White 1980; Sowell 1985; Loury 1985; Cleaver 1987). This constructing, according to Cornell West (1994), drew its strength from extending the crudest of common thought to know this violence.

But my book suggests something different. I examine both discourses, conservative and liberal, and document that the supposed oppositional voice—liberalism—was complicit in this constructing. I chronicle a dominant strand of liberal thought in the 1980s and 1990s—one I have termed "agency-oriented liberalism"—and demonstrate that it aggressively narrated this violence in newspapers, magazines, TV news, and local policy pronouncements, and reproduced key notions of conservative presentation. Proponents of this "agency-oriented liberalism" appeared quite different from conservatives, speaking about "black-on-black violence" as concerned and impassioned readers and helpers. They ruminated with pleasure about black community promise and potential and narrated a tragedy of senseless violence. They even articulated the "reality" of racism and economic inequality, forces conservatives supposedly refused to acknowledge. But I suggest that their articulations also communicated and thereby underscored a central causal factor for this violence: local values and culture. Offering a more complex rendition of social problem, commitment to causation and a style of presentation ultimately communicated the importance of "a people's" ways, lifestyles, and values. I contend these liberal articulations were equally important to creating the systematic way America has produced—sociologically, scientifically, imaginatively—"black-on-black violence" as one societal problem.

The Work

There are many recognized ways to conduct a discourse analysis to anchor social constructionist inquiry (Lincoln 1989; Yin 1994). My study of the two discourses, taking a new and novel approach, highlights the effect of a key resource to shape their content: imagined mental spaces (see author's note). I follow the recent "spatial turn" in the social sciences to chronicle this space's influence in these formations. This space, Henri Lefebvre's (1984) imagined mental maps used in discourse, routinely builds notions about social issues, using such space as a signifier. Any serious discourse analysis, to Lefebvre, needs to illuminate this influence. Lefebvre's spaces in the imagination (for example, "the ghetto," "the slum," and "the underclass neighborhood") provide meanings to understand social issues. Their content helps display the nature of people (for example, "black kids" and "black families") and processes (for example, "welfare persistence" and "local drug-selling") that ground presentations of social issues. Space, in this sense, is a creating force inseparable from language's influence. To Lefebvre (1984), research has been for too long "content to see . . . an apparently neutral, objective, fixed, transparent, [and] innocent . . . space" removed from the power of language and discourse.

My focus is thus one kind of space that Lefebvre (1984) identifies, "representations of space." This kind of space has received little treatment as an applied building ingredient in discourse. Lefebvre recognizes three important concepts in this area: representations of space, spatial practices, and representational spaces. They are the "triad" of processes that reveal how space as a made product imperceptibly affects people's everyday seeing and living. The first concept, representations of space, involves spaces of the imagination that mediate "seeing" the world and its things. The second and third concepts, spatial practices and representational spaces, are actual physical things. While spatial practices are the ongoing activities that reproduce/rearrange meaning-filled physical spaces, representational spaces are those physical spaces themselves. What a space becomes as something represented (representational spaces) will often closely correspond with this sense of space in the common imagining (representations of space).

Our focus, Lefebvre's representations of space, is crafted and codified (often institutionalized) maps in the imagination to know the world. These created "spaces of scientists . . . urbanists, technocratic subdividers and social engineers" present worlds from distinctive viewpoints. In his example, urban planners offer numerous imagined spaces—ghettos, slums, central business districts, and urban renewal zones—that provide objects for these practitioners to manipulate. Others in diverse endeavors also offer imagined spaces that choreograph the visual for political purposes: architects, sociologists, historic preservationists, geographers, Democrats, Republicans, liberals, conservatives, businesspeople, and labor activists. To paraphrase Lefebvre, not only does every society produce its own imagined space, so too does every kind of specialist and interest group.

Such mental spaces may or may not serve the purposes of politically emancipatory projects. But they always project undeniable, absolute realities for people to "know through." Through them, people are asked to know places, institutions, processes, and indeed reality itself. Such spaces always project fact and neutrality but, quoting Lefebvre (1984, 107), "ride roughshod . . . over the world . . . and support established [visions] on the one hand and den[y] the possibility of knowing [other visions] on the other." To Lefebvre, such spaces always stand in for the real world as simplified and caricatured constructs. Simplifying the world, the essence of advancing political projects and representing complex landscapes and worlds, is done both deliberately and as a reflection of habit.

These points made, my discourse analysis focuses on their foundation, their "fields of understanding" (fig. 1). This is the made reality of forces, people, and processes that ground and anchor presentations of issues (that is, their "context"). Objects in this "field" comprise the contextual setting that supports issue-specific discussions, in our case, this violence. Thus, notions of "black-on-black violence" required elaborate setups of people, places, and processes that stood in as supportive realities. Every discussion of black–on–black violence, liberal or conservative, relied on these setups. This frame to stage realities was inseparable from offerings of plot and theme. These fields of understanding, as conceptual anchor, assumed the status of everyday reality that supported causative assertions about this violence.

This notion of discourse potentially lessens focus and internal unity. Rich contextualizing in discourse analysis, to Norman Fairclough (1992), reduces focus on central subject. But this tack recognizes the complexity and richness of discourse (see Wagner-Pacifici, 1994). Discourse becomes much more than mere articulations about topical issues. The analogy of a puzzle is instructive. Making the final image (the discourse) requires making and strategically situating the multitude of pieces. Without these pieces, final image could not be assembled and provided clear meaning. My analysis of these discourses thus emphasizes the situating of this social issue (Mikhail Bakhtin's "staging" of issues). This focus has a rich tradition in discourse studies, notably in the writing of Mikhail Bakhtin (1981) and Kenneth Burke (1969) and more recently Norman Fairclough (1992), Robin Wagner-Pacifici (1994), and Jonathan Potter (1996).

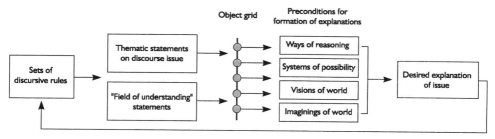

Figure 1. Content of Discourse. (Source: derived by author)

The time frame of analysis, 1980 to the present, captures a crucial era in American race relations, the current. Urban African Americans became more stigmatized and marginalized in a stepped-up rhetorical assault on their ways, values, and lifestyles. At the rhetorical level, the rise of Ronald Reagan and his portrayal of "this group" ushered in this era. Discussions of welfare queens, the undeserving poor, poverty freeloaders, and aberrant ghetto values marshaled a public hostility to African Americans whose institutionalization in policy (for instance, reduced food stamps, workfare, enterprise zones, end of the Comprehensive Employment and Training Act) continues. At the material level, black ghettos in urban America have experienced a sharp deterioration (David Wilson 1996; Wacquant 1994a). In this context, "black-on-black violence" appeared as a new, "raced" social ill that everyone supposedly had to realize and respond to. This construction continues unabated today.

The Power and Nature of Discourse

Why a focus on discourse to understand this violence? Many in urban studies and geography now view discourse as central to making understandings about such social processes (see Short 1996, 1999; Jonas and Wilson 1999). It is suggested people know the world and act upon it not through brute empirical interrogations but through coded "readings." People always "confront" representations rather than a real world in gazes, conversations, and interactions: these powerfully stand in for the world. In this context, discourses offer realities and suppress rich possibilities for "seeing" alternatives, trapping its contentions in its own web of "truths."

Discourses, ensnaring and coercive, construct worlds for popular consumption under the guise of being simple narrations of reality.

Befitting this recognition, the discourse notion has emerged as the fundamental challenge to the foundational premises of knowledge generation (see Mumby 1993). The best known discussion of this challenge, Jean François Lyotard's *The Postmodern Condition* (1984), examines the current status of knowledge. Lyotard argues that knowledge is less a neutral body of "fact" than discourse-driven contentions that legitimate their own status and existence. Lyotard's discourse is a knowledge-ensnaring cage that both makes and cordons off understandings from criticism. Discourse, a complex apparatus, is inseparable from producing and protecting "facts," seamlessly "writing" the world as a mechanism controlled by its users. To produce knowledge, to Lyotard, is to use discourse to construct realities.

With this emphasis on discourse as investigative object, it has been defined in different ways but perhaps most thoughtfully by Peter Goodrich (1987). He defines discourse as views and interests on topics communicated through terms and concepts (compare Wagner-Pacifici 1994; Lemke 1995; Short 1999). Discourses map swaths of subject matter across the enormity of societal knowledge that impart shape, form, and content to reality. They offer elaborate and rich presentations of reality that always mediate people's interrogations of the world. Whether people know it or not, their understandings always reflect the influence of discourse. One can thus talk fruitfully about discourses on education, rurality, child rearing, Americana, immigrants, urban violence, urban policy, progressive politics, reactionary politics, and many others.

Yet to Goodrich discourses are surprisingly complex constructions. They "speak" directly to specific issues (for example, crime, pollution, poverty) but always construct elaborate worlds of people, places, and processes to make their messages coherent. This construction of "support worlds," on the one hand, fulfills the crucial need to "stage" truths about specific themes, but also connects to the lifeline of other discourses as support constructs. These support worlds of people and processes, in other words, are necessary inclusions to make issue-specific presentations appear logical and borrow from the stages established in other discourses to infuse their "grounding" with legitimacy. Thus discourses of "black-on-black violence" built elaborate realities about the nature of this process but also connected to other 1980s discourses on drugs, public housing, public schools, welfare policy, and others. Goodrich terms this process of borrowing "intertextuality" (from Bakhtin), with discourses continuously melding into the content of other discourses.

Goodrich's work, of course, borrows extensively from the insights of master analysts of discourse, and should be seen as one fertile body of work in a historical continuum. There has been a rich history of research in discourse, in particular by Raymond Williams, Michel Foucault, Mikhail Bakhtin, and Kenneth Burke. Each studies discourse within different theoretical frameworks and across different subject matters. Most prominently, Raymond Williams examined discourses of locally constructed everydays; Michel Foucault examined dominant discourses across disciplines of psychiatry, medicine, and criminology; Mikhail Bakhtin studied discourses in literature, particularly that of Rabelais; and, much earlier, Kenneth Burke examined discourses in everyday thought and belief. There is much that separates these thinkers, but what unifies them is the recognition of language use as an exercise of power and politics.

Discourses emerge as ensnaring worlds, with "readers" positioned as eavesdropping observers. People are drawn into worlds and dragged along paths littered with icons, images, and metaphorical props. Along this path, narrated things fitted together nudge people to "see" certain realities. This path, made the "truth" of the world in uncompromising objectivity, immerses people in "staged realities." Wherever one "looks" along this path, self-fulfilling signs function as a series of proofs. Produced worlds never remove themselves from their producers, invariably reflecting their tools, strategies, politics, and ways. Any potential evidence that contradicts the offered "reality" is purged from the path. Discourses, nourished by affirming realities, are boldly supported; these worlds are crucial to making "truths" appear logical and rational.

Discourses are thus sources of power and persuasion, "taking over" the world and offering symbolic universes to produce realities for public consumption. On the one hand, they open up creative possibility for critical reflection. Through them one creative slant on reality is offered. But they also constrict, creating perceptions that make certain actions thinkable and others not. Discourses thus impose webs of circular meanings that constrain opportunities to work beyond this meaning. They project symbolic cages that build bars around senses of reality, placing gazes within discrete and confining visions. Objects and processes are clasped to staked-out moral and cultural centers and peripheries. Worlds are presented that allow narrativists to situate themselves at "the authorial standpoint."

As Michel Foucault (1971) puts it, people end up both masters and slaves to discourse. People are free to draw on discourse, use it at their convenience, and tailor it to specific conditions, but always submit to its boundedness. Discourses free us and ensnare us, enable us to express ourselves and speak our truths, yet constrict our thoughts and imaginings. To paraphrase Foucault (1971), people express their thoughts in words that they have not mastered, enclosing these in verbal forms whose historical dimensions they are unaware of, with people believing that speech is their servant and not realizing that they submit themselves to its demands. Discourse is thus a communicative instrument that enables but also disables. Every time we grasp the world through discourse, to Foucault, we gain and lose.

Discourses, it follows, have an enormous capacity to wield oppression. To Norman Fairclough (1992), discourses are the modern alternative to material violence and overt oppression. The game in complex societies, to Fairclough, is to make and manage rather than to overtly punish and discipline. With diverse populations and intense competition for resources and power, taming through producing and managing knowledge is continuous. For discourses can make inequity seem necessary, make hatred and violence rational, and render opinion and subjectivities mere technical matters. In the name of upholding civic values and protecting cultural integrity, marginalizing people can appear justified and necessary. In this sense, discourses can normalize the most perverse disciplining of people as a public can accept and even embrace inequality.

But before discourse becomes influential it must struggle for dominance. Discourses are always involved in advancing their reality and attacking alternatives. Mikhail Bakhtin (1981) describes this as the implicit dialogue with other points of view, the simultaneity of putting together visions and decimating others. Discourses communicate realities but also speak about the delusions of alternatives. "Reading" one offered reality conveys two messages: what exists and what does not. This is the simultaneity of affirmation and rebuke that makes discourses instruments of power. Successful discourses are accorded the status of truth and fact, failed ones the status of opinion and assertion. Only one is enabled through consensus to control and manage. Winners strike out and deepen common understandings through discourse, losers pursue transgression and subversion. But always there is contestation; the struggle is to control comprehension.

Yet discourses in all their communicative possibilities are not hatched out of thin air: They, to Bruce Lincoln (1989), depend upon rather than stand independent from the world. Lincoln means that discourses must hook into prevailing common sense—current understandings and perceptions—that is the context for offering discourse. Successful discourses persuasively follow from and extend sense of the world to expand understanding. Is there much room for creativity and change within these constraints? Bakhtin and De Certeau say yes and I agree. As has recently been shown, common understandings can be extended many ways. In the process, common understandings of people and processes can be bolstered or subverted. For example, post-1960s gains in civil rights, gay rights, and women's rights have followed from discourses that extended common sense to fruitfully confront bigotry. But, alternatively, bigotry could have been extended in these situations to swallow up these movements as had been done in the past.

A final point in this section: I assert that discourse analysis can contribute much to our understanding of the "black-on-black violence" issue. Most studies on this topic have examined it as a given reality and not as a racialized construct. For example, Bruce Marino, Vincent J. Roscigno, and Patricia L. McCall (1998) examine "black-on-black violence" as a new and perplexing social crisis. They make this violence an objective reality and explain it by both structural (globalization, deindustrialization) and agency (bounded youth choice) influences. Their explanation, purportedly unlike others, is a nuanced one that incorporates context, circumstance, and human action. They propose a complex causality as the antidote to prevailing agency-based explanations. But an incompleteness looms: they fail to recognize "black-on-black violence" as a socially constituted understanding. Marino et al., in other words, never interrogate what this violence is as a mainstream comprehension, treating it as an outgrowth of complex societal change but leaving its core existence as a kind of understanding unexplored.

Similarly, William Oliver (1989) explains "black-on-black violence" with reference to broad-based societal forces. Again, "black-on-black violence" is accepted as a given empirical reality. His portrait shows the structural pressures placed on urban blacks and their supposed frequently dysfunctional adaptation to such pressures. Unlike Marino et al., causation is placed principally in societal processes: societal racism, economic deindustrialization, and lack of effective government redistributive mechanisms. Local culture in inner cities, decimated by these forces, renders these neighborhoods ill-equipped to "mainstream" kids. Local culture, identified as a fundamental shaper of youth values and aspirations, mediates the effect of these societal forces on youth. To Oliver, deindustrialization, high unemployment, and institutional racism ravage local culture, which creates hopelessness and high rates of violence.

One study to date, by James Nadell (1995), has examined "black-on-black violence" in the U.S. context as a social construction. Yet there is a problem here as well that needs discussion. This study, an important break with standard research practice, fails to fully examine the breadth of the construction. Nadell analyzes this issue as a direct set of thematic articulations. Nadell's discourse is little more than a constructed set of pronouncements on a subject matter, "black-on-black violence," that ignores its crucial contextual situating. This is a serious omission. Nadell indicts the mainstream commercial media as organizers of a discourse whose statements about this violence (in movies) make the issue an oppressive, power-laden tool. Nadell suggests that this discourse suppresses alternative conceptions of this violence in favor of an agency-based, conservative one. This construction, to Nadell, reinforces a popular notion of inner cities as vile places with dysfunctional kids.

What is undeveloped in this work is the contextual richness of the discourse, something my study focuses on. As Robin Wagner-Pacifici (1994) notes, an important part of discourses is diverse representations that situate their topical matter in enabling fields of understanding (see fig. 1). This collection of images, values, meanings, and "facts" assigned to people, places, and processes in discourse "platforms" discussion of issues. Thus, as we will discover, the conservative and liberal constructions of "black-on-black violence" commonly relied on constructions of black youth, black inner cities, underclass culture, black families, and black politicians as foundational elements (the field of understanding) to impart meaning. These continuously discussed elements in discourse took backstage to direct articulations about the violence but grounded sense of causes and culprits. These discourses, then, will be revealed as sets of disparate elements creatively tied together to support issue-specific pronouncements.

The Existence of Violence

A final important introductory point: what has been the actual reality of inner city violence involving African Americans after 1980? Much evidence suggests that this violence in inner cities did escalate. Proof of this escalating violence in inner cities comes in two forms, narrative accounts and statistical data, that I now briefly document. But we should never forget that possibilities for this representing were endless. Mainstream "voices" of influence could have represented this violence in numerous ways, emphasizing, for example, class, poverty, oppression, hopelessness, human denigration, economic deindustrialization, and impacts of globalization. These voices, instead, coalesced around mainstream notions and stereotypes of race. Like all social issues, I suggest, there was a reality here but it was multi-interpretable. This reality, always understood through a competition of discourses, forever made it a vehicle for political ambitions. This point recognized, I discuss the actual reality of this violence.

First, different narratives of this violence (mainstream, nonmainstream, for example conservative, liberal, Marxist, black separatist) all documented rising violence and changing inner cities. All agreed inner cities suffered from accelerated deterioration reflected in increased drugs (especially crack cocaine), declining living conditions, vanishing jobs, mounting youth frustration, and growing unemployment. Drug selling, drug addiction, lessened job opportunities, and economic instability were universally acknowledged as more prevalent. Selling crack cocaine, the new scourge of inner cities, emerged as the new employer of youth and adults. The result was increased crime: purse snatching, car theft, assault, and murder. There were vast differences in proposed causes for and real realities about this violence, but its increase was never a point of contention. Hundreds of quotes support this reality (all were constructions and many were caricatures and embellishments), but let me simply offer two from conservative and liberal political positions, respectively.

> Bystanders are increasingly the victims of Bay Area violence and what a San Francisco police officer calls "little brains and big guns." "And kids with guns are the worst, [homicide Inspector Jeff Brosch] said. "A 40 year-old ex-convict with a weapon doesn't particularly concern me . . . But a kid of 14 or so who is armed scares the heck out of me . . . They have little brains and big guns. (Martinez 1994, A-1)

> It[']s worse. [Yesterday] they sniped me. I couldn't get out of the way in time 'cause it was an automatic rifle. I knew it was an automatic rifle 'cause I hear it every day. You have to be careful coming into the building. They could be right around the corner. (Wilkerson 1989, A-12)

> [Things are so bad here]. We need . . . To stand up and be men against gang violence. We must stand up and tell our young men to study violence no more. That violence is self-defeating, and we are killing ourselves." (Davidson and Ricktenwald 1984, 1)

> "We care [about the violence]—[but] that message is often overpowered by the media images of street-corner drug wars and "gangsta" rappers. . . . among blacks [like myself], there is a rising sense of alarm and outrage at the robberies, muggings, drive-by shootings and murders that have made crime the nation's No. 1 concern." (White and Walker 1994)

Statistical data also testifies to this escalation. A sample year, 1984, reveals that every category of violent crime in urban America increased and

TABLE 2

U.S. Crime Rates by Racial Distribution

Offense	White (%)	Black (%)	American Indian or Indian or Alaskan Native (%)	Asian or Pacific Islander (%)
Violent crime	**48.6**	**50.2**	**0.7**	**0.6**
Murder and non-negligent manslaughter	46.7	52.0	0.6	0.8
Forcible rape	46.4	52.3	0.7	0.6
Robbery	35.2	63.7	0.4	0.7
Aggravated assault	56.1	42.5	0.8	0.6
Property Crime	**66.1**	**32.0**	**1.1**	**0.9**
Burglary	66.2	32.4	0.8	0.6
Larceny-theft	66.2	31.7	1.2	1.0
Motor vehicle theft	63.6	34.6	0.9	0.9
Arson	74.2	24.3	0.8	0.7

Source: W. J. Wilson 1987.

disproportionately involved African Americans (see table 2). Blacks constituted less than 35 percent of the population in U.S. cities but were targets for over 50 percent of all violent crime. Blacks in 1984 represented more than half of those arrested for murders and non-negligent manslaughter, more than half of those arrested for forcible rape, and 64 percent of those arrested for robbery. Only one in nine persons in America was black in 1984, but nearly one in two arrested for murder and non-negligent manslaughter was black (W. J. Wilson 1987). At the same time, 41 percent of all murder victims in cities were black (W. J. Wilson 1987). In 1984, one in twenty-four black households nationally had a member raped, robbed, or assaulted: The figure was one in forty-two for white households (Page 1987).

In New York City, 85 percent of black homicide victims in 1984 were killed by other blacks (Page 1987). The bulk of these killings were in the South Bronx and Brooklyn, areas where poverty and hopelessness were massive. In Chicago, youth murders that year were more than five times the national metropolitan-wide (city and suburb) average (*Chicago Tribune* 1984). Chicago's predominantly black South Side, the focus, also housed the city's highest number of poor and malnourished children (*Chicago Tribune* 1984). In 1985, murder was the most common death for black males aged fifteen to forty-four across the country (W. J. Wilson 1987). Black Americans who died from this violence that year equaled the number of black servicemen killed during twelve years of the Vietnam War (Page 1988).

Surveys of inner city residents substantiate the reality of this escalating violence. A 1989 survey of more than one thousand Chicago school students found that 74 percent had witnessed a murder, shooting, stabbing, or robbery in their lifetime (Kotulak 1990) (see table 3). Forty-six percent of the youths had been victims of rape, shooting, stabbing, robbery, or some other violent act. During Mayor Harold Washington's tenure in Chicago, 1983–87, when possibilities for improved race relations seemed brightest, 58 percent of residents felt that crime conditions had recently worsened (Page 1987). In 1980, violent crime in the United States soared 13 percent, the precursor to a more violent decade across America that was particularly acute in U.S. inner cities (*Chicago Sun-Times* 1981a). In America's inner cities, with intensifying patterns of racial segregation, William Julius Wilson (1987) suggests, violent crime here was increasingly intraracial.

This violence, not surprisingly, was concentrated in intense-poverty areas. New York City's South Bronx and Bedford Stuyvesant, Philadelphia's "North Philly" and "South Philly," Cleveland's Hough, Los Angeles's South Central, and Chicago's Wentworth area were notable (see Simon 1981; Gailey 1986; Freligh 1998). In 1980, their poverty and unemployment rates were more than twice the national average, and rates of substandard housing and job loss from ten years earlier were more than three times the national average (U.S. Census Bureau 1980b). These were the areas where economic deprivation and human suffering were among the highest in the United States (see William Oliver 1989). It is no coincidence that these five cities—New York, Philadelphia, Cleveland, Los

TABLE 3

Chicago Children and Violence★

Witnessed murder, shooting, stabbing or robbery	74 percent
Victim of rape, shooting, stabbing, robbery, or other violent act	46 percent
Witnessed a shooting	39 percent
Witnessed a stabbing	35 percent
Witnessed a murder	24 percent

★As percentage of one thousand south-side and southwest-side schoolchildren.

Source: Chicago Tribune 1984

Angeles, Chicago—were ranked in the top ten highest murder cities be-tween 1979 and 1984.

Chicago's desperately poor Wentworth area is illustrative. This zone of burned-out housing and widespread poverty was the poorest urban area in the United States in 1980. Containing the massive Robert Taylor Homes, a complex of twenty-eight sixteen-story public housing build-ings on ninety-two acres, all 25,000 residents lived at or below the poverty level. In 1980, median family income and employment was less than one-half and one-third the city average (W. J. Wilson 1987). In this four-square-mile district in 1983, 11 percent of city murders, 9 percent of rapes, and 10 percent of aggravated assaults occurred. Putting aside grue-some descriptions of this setting that cast it as "killing fields" and "places of core incivility" (Beverly 1991), here were disproportionate poverty and violence that few could deny. As had always been the case, where there were high concentrations of poverty, there were also disproportionate amounts of violence regardless of people's race or ethnicity.

The Goal

My investigation builds on recent work that examines the racializing of social issues in Anglo-America (see Peter Jackson 1989; Pinckney 1990; Wacquant 1994a, 1994b). I follow what some have termed the new cultural political economy school, others the new racial economy per-spective, that recognizes the power of discourse, space, representation, economy, and authorial voice to build current social realities as preludes to advancing political designs. I work from the thesis that machineries of representation as political-economic tools are inseparable from the construction and rise of politically expedient problems, fears, and issues in society. This constructing of "black-on-black violence" as an issue, I suggest, pivoted around use of a key resource, humanly crafted space. This essence, used as so many imaginary spaces in discourse, gave form and character to diverse people and processes that as a kind of contextual framing normalized this rendition of violence.

This study is not an exercise in phenomenology or in expunging demons from common thought; it reveals how a public issue in America—"black-on-black violence"—was made, complete with villains, ominous forces, and victims. If we accept that a dominant reality on this issue was made by discourse, what was this reality? How was it made? And what resources were used in this constructing? At issue is the complex means by which this issue was racialized along common understandings and transmitted through everyday life. At work across the wealth of U.S. cities, I contend, was a politics of reality-making that extended understandings of urban black youth in bold but established ways. Like any social issue constructed a certain way, its content had ties to its makers' goals and needs that I now discuss.

2

Postwar Representations
of Urban Black Youth, 1950–1980

I initially propose that this post-1980 "black-on-black violence" discourse was not hatched out of thin air. Postwar representations of urban black youth on diverse issues prior to 1980 set the stage for this creation that I now review. These kids, pre-1980, were coded continuously as threatening and central to city woes that were crucial context. Diverse discourses accomplished this coding: on urban decline, neighborhood downgrading, urban renewal, public housing, and public education, among others. This prominent "black-on-black violence" vision, as revealed later, borrowed and built on these pre-1980 understandings. Dominant representations of these kids and their communities pre-1980, always simple and easily comprehensible, made them convenient political figures. This caricature, as will be shown, flowed from numerous sources: politicians, TV commentators, magazine essayists, newspaper reporters, academics, and pundits.

But the forces that pushed this representing also need clarification. Prominent in this representing, I suggest, have been attempts to explain and reverse a perplexing problem in mainstream American thought: a sense of declining cities as stages for profit accumulation and symbolic American values. U.S. cities have, since their inception, been economic engines and places of rich symbolic significance. Cities have fueled local and national economies as staging grounds for production and real-estate investment and have been dominant symbols of U.S. capitalist virility. Numerous writers and academics have noted this significance, and I add detail to their thesis in this chapter. Thomas Cochran (2001, 2), executive direc-

21

tor of the U.S. Conference of Mayors, sums up this recognition: "U.S. cities [have been] the economic engines that drive this nation and that have pro-duced . . . incredible economic growth." U.S. cities, to Cochran, have sustained America's materialist realities and imagined destinies. What American capitalism is and has wanted to be, in his words, has been inti-mately bound up with cities.

But U.S. cities, in my assertion, declined quickly and dramatically in the eyes of many after 1945, and had to be explained and reversed. A fun-damental part of the societal engagement with cities in the postwar years, explanations for decline and ameliorative policy interventions, offered a prominent urban folk-devil who would be progressively embellished: black kids and communities. The specifics of this constructing fluctuated over time but never wavered in blaming these kids and places for city problems. These inviting targets, lacking political clout and social stand-ing, could be easily villainized. Against this backdrop, the "black-on-black violence" discourse emerged shortly thereafter. This post-1980 render-ing, borrowing and building on these understandings of black youth, had intimate ties to the past.

Postwar Suburbanization and City Decline I, 1950–1967

Nineteen-fifties and 1960s suburbanization and urban decline were sub-stantial and concerned the American public. By 1970, 54.2 percent of the country's metropolitan population lived in suburbs, an increase of more than 30 percent from twenty years earlier (Judd 1979). Suburbanization was an institutionally-driven solution to a 1940s national economic malaise and uncertain postwar social order. After World War II, weak local and national economies and uncertain social stability needed bolstering; this development was the potential panacea. At the same time, cities, his-torically ideal for real-estate investment, industrial production, and social reproduction of labor, had aged (Harvey 1981, 1989). Once-fertile ter-rains for investment had become traps for real-estate and corporate capi-tal. In this context, suburban property development, utility extension, housing construction, and mortgage lending were strategic.

As now chronicled, a mind-boggling set of government supports fueled this unfolding: Federal Housing Administration and Veterans Affairs mortgage loan programs, the secondary mortgage market, thrift lenders, the Federal Deposit Insurance Corporation, and local tax abatement programs (see Walker 1981; Palen 1995). Each helped make spaces that could seamlessly absorb new investment and traditional bourgeois values. These programs and policies fueled consumption of land and housing, production of buildings and neighborhoods, and reproduction of existing social relations. The federal government, willing to tackle economic malaise, propelled suburbanization through these programs. Constructing suburban space, paraphrasing Richard Walker (1981), became the "societal solution" to impending economic crisis facing America.

This 1950s and 1960s afflicting suburbanization (and accelerated black migration to cities) reordered the popular imagining of cities. It fostered a dominant postwar city image: the ailing minority landscape. In image, production-based cities had deteriorated and had become voraciously consumptive. Black ghettos, Puerto Rican neighborhoods, deteriorating central business districts, and struggling downtowns were new and growing formations populating cities. Once proud, strong, and traditional neighborhoods and districts had given way to new communities and spaces that unapologetically used public resources. Cities were going to hell, in this crystallizing imagery, and conditions seemed unlikely to improve. As Minneapolis mayor Hubert Humphrey and writer Michael Harrington noted:

> What's wrong with our cities? . . . [S]lums, rotten broken-down areas, are the ulcers which may develop into the cancer that will continue the physical and economic structure of the industrial city. Slum areas are the extravagances that eat up our revenues and destroy our strength . . . Either we lick the slums or the slums will destroy our city. (Humphrey 1948, 12–13)

> There is a new type of slum. Its citizens are the internal migrants, the Negroes, the poor whites from the farms, the Puerto Ricans. They join the failures of the old ethnic culture and form an entirely different kind of neighborhood . . . All of them arrive at a time of housing short-

age . . . and thus it is hard to escape even when income rises. But, above all, these people do not participate in the culture of aspiration that was the vitality of the ethnic slum. (Harrington 1962, 46)

Writer George Sternlieb's popular essays also illustrate the media's projection of U.S. cities as growing poverty repositories (1966, 1970). To Sternlieb, cities were evolving into residual storehouses for poor kids and families. "At present," to Sternlieb, "the problem is more and more that of maintaining any middle class . . . The city as an institution cannot survive in any desirable form merely by serving as a reservation for those who cannot make it to the suburbs" (1966, 64). The dilemma, to Sternlieb, was the presence of a people that taxed housing stocks, created overcrowding, spawned slums, and chased away middle-income families. Comments by *U.S News and World Report* in 1966 also reflect this concern about poor minorities. They note: "if present trends continue, Negroes will outnumber whites in 8 of the 10 biggest cities in the U.S.—or come close to it— by the year 2000" (in Beauregard 1993, 171).

Black youth and communities were placed at the core of the "urban minority question." These kids, in narrative, typically roamed city streets, chased whites and investment out of downtowns, and left sinking neighborhoods and districts in their wake. These community-damaging kids were contagious and repulsed non-poor blacks, industrialists, and investors from cities. Actions of these kids, in short, reverberated powerfully across the cities. These places were being rapidly colonized by blacks and being taken over by growing hordes of black kids. These kids, in the words of Edward Banfield (1968), "were present-oriented . . . culturally destroying their communities and cities . . . but refused to see it."

The narrated dilemma was simple: kids unable to integrate into city social and cultural life. These kids, thrown into complex modern conditions, failed to adjust to modern industrial life and became nonpurposeful and dandyist. Cities became alien cultural terrain to them: disillusionment and aimlessness led to community destructive acts (ghettoizing schools, playgrounds, streets, parks) that hastened neighborhood decline. As *Senior Scholastic* and *Fortune* (in Beauregard 1993, 169, 171) claimed in 1970: "many of the blacks who have moved to the cities came from rural regions, lacking the education and training necessary to crack the increasingly specialized urban job market . . ." The result was a "Negro [and youth] Problem [that] represents a crisis within a crisis, a specific and acute syndrome in a body already ill from more general disorders."

But real-estate interests, government, and America fought hard to maintain this wealth-creating mechanism and national icon, the city. Urban resuscitation was planned amidst the intensification of urban change. Government in the 1950s began its first postwar foray into urban revitalization: public housing and urban renewal. These, not surprisingly, sought to recapture urban economic bases and tax bases. Both programs, rooted in strategies of state-sanctioned isolation of poor minorities, were acutely spatial undertakings. They manipulated land uses across downtowns to maximize city growth and development. These were the goals to which Housing Secretary Robert C. Weaver (1966, 43) spoke when he noted that "urban renewal perform[s] . . . indispensable . . . functions for preserving our cities." Here people and land uses that devalued property were to be cordoned off, albeit provided roughly proximate locations to before.

Public housing had been initiated on a small scale in 1934; fewer than twenty U.S. cities contained public housing in 1940 (James Q. Wilson 1966). But after 1955, the program was given a new urgency with the public sense of deteriorating cities and problem minorities. Between 1949 and 1967, more than six hundred public housing projects were launched in some seven hundred cities (Jakle and Wilson 1992). Over half were to house more than five hundred families. In planning schemes, central portions of downtowns were targeted for destruction and public housing construction. Many projects were designed to capture those displaced from nearby urban renewal projects; others were envisioned as new neighborhoods for the poor (James Q. Wilson 1966). By 1970, over 450 public housing projects in U.S. cities had been built. Typically, projects were monstrous in scale (usually over ten acres in size and housing thousands of people) and horrifyingly concentrative of people.

But the program offered with much fanfare soon blew up in government's face. As early as the late 1950s, public housing was being criticized by both conservatives and liberals as slum-sustaining, paternalistic, and

welfare-perpetuating (see Packard 1960; Jacobs 1961). It flagrantly isolated and stigmatized poor people to a degree that embarrassed politicians. But because public housing so effectively walled off "dangerous"
and "property-value-threatening" people, a perceived necessity by
growth elites in cities, its use continued. Never had such an unpopular but
functionally efficient program gone so far. In 1965, the program housed
more than two million people and every state had some public housing
(Friedman 1980). By 1970, the program sheltered nearly 1 percent of the
nation's population, and every city over 250,000 except one had public
housing in place (Solomon 1974). In 1975, New York City operated
116,000 units, Philadelphia 22,900, Chicago 38,600, Baltimore 16,200,
and Atlanta 24,700 (Jakle and Wilson 1992). In the 1980s, public housing
constituted 15 percent of the total housing stock in Atlanta, 10 percent in
Baltimore, and 9 percent in Philadelphia (Jakle and Wilson 1992).

Discussions of public housing's failures, not surprisingly, often invoked
problem black kids and households. These people, packed into sterile and
stigmatized complexes in desolate surroundings, became a central issue on
the topic. The attack focused on the sense of a distinctive group's worlds
and ways. Purportedly deformed and defective, they were rendered culturally dysfunctional and ritually destructive of property and social stability.
Whatever they occupied and touched, it was suggested, became downgraded. Not surprisingly, then, these blocks of housing and their neighborhoods soon fell into a dramatic decline. These were Ed Banfield's
(1968) "lower class kids"— "impulsive" and "present oriented"—who
"dropped out of school . . . had illegitimate children . . . were unemployed and unemployable." Products of a culture that spurned middle-class
values, this youth had to spend more time sacrificing and practicing self-
improvement.

Also in the 1950s and 1960s, America sought to renew U.S. cities
with urban renewal. This program, begun in the early 1930s, was re-
asserted in the 1950s as a bold way to reorder cities. Here, again, was the
proverbial whip to lash into shape a hemorrhaging economic base and social order. Urban economies from New York to Los Angeles were faltering, social order purportedly disappearing, and demolition and spatial
remaking were proposed as the solution. Society and the state, serving

as assessor and intervener, offered urban renewal as a progressive undertaking rooted in systematic physical destruction. Blighted buildings and neighborhoods were to be razed and replaced by more optimal land uses. The city, now supposedly soft and undisciplined, required a stern response. Paraphrasing Philadelphia Urban Renewal Director William Rafsky (1978), America had to repudiate softness that had crept into this once virile economic instrument; nothing else would do.

Between 1955 and 1970, over $3 billion in federal aid was earmarked for this program (Weicher 1970). It would, to William Rafsky (1978), "demolish the cancer of blight" and clear land for new housing and business investment. And in the 1960s, urban renewal was enhanced. Earlier projects had sometimes provided moderate-or middle-income housing; planners after 1965 increasingly opted for glamorous business and financial projects. Such development would supposedly yield more dramatic results than the more modest "welfarist" schemes (Teaford 1990). As part of this development, amendments to urban renewal law gave cities greater flexibility to implement redevelopment in 1959 and 1961; many cities responded to the new opportunity.

These projects were stunning in their obliteration of entire neighborhoods. A relentless modernism infused these schemes, destroying the old and obsolete and replacing it with the supposed new and efficient. Here was the planning implementation of Lewis Mumford's call to take city parts and "cart them away and begin all over" (in Fang 1998). In New York and Boston, zealous administrators like Robert Moses and John Collins demolished established neighborhoods and replaced them with bleak, repetitious housing slabs. In Newark and Pittsburgh, central portions of downtown were gutted and replaced with sterile office high-rises (Montgomery 1966; Harold Kaplan 1966). Cleveland and Detroit experienced massive destruction of many downtown neighborhoods that left vacant lots and blocks (Teaford 1990).

But by the mid-1960s, urban renewal's rambunctious destructiveness had proven too destructive. The programs demolished many more homes than they had built and had displaced more people and activities than they relocated (Boyer 1983). In Pittsburgh, urban renewal as the city's dominant postwar policy tool razed more than 3,700 buildings, relocated more than 1,800 businesses, and uprooted more than 5,000 families (Fitzpatrick 2000). Housing and buildings were typically replaced by utilitarian-style shopping complexes and office towers. In St. Louis, the shockingly slow Mill Creek Valley Project embarrassed city officials and revealed the difficulties of redeveloping severely disinvested land. Mill Creek was called by the *New York Times* (in Teaford 1990) "the questionable spectacle of one of the country's most unsuccessful redevelopment programs." Buffalo's Ellicott project, the model of delay and inaction, began in 1954 and by late 1964 contained only six new single-family homes. The project displaced 2,200 black families in a 161-acre area and proved unattractive for middle-income black reoccupation; few wanted to live near slums.

To explain urban renewal's failure, many experts not surprisingly blamed the time-tested enigmatic entities: black neighborhoods and black kids. As government seized homes and land, built profit opportunities for developers, and deepened socioeconomic isolation, residents were fingered as unnecessarily resistant and unwilling to change. The scapegoating was blunt. Urban renewal was supposedly innovative but it typically engaged socially-disorganized and community-destroying people and kids who confounded matters. Recent comments by the St. Louis Home Project and the Center for Reclaiming America reflect the continuance of this scapegoating:

Urban renewal has always created . . . what it frequently demolished . . . social decay, chaos, and dysfunctional neighborhoods. Laclede Town [like other renewal projects] was stuck with murder, assault, rape, shattered windows, cars that get stomped on each night until no one can live there. [With renewal] students move out. Businessmen move out. The African Americans remain. (St. Louis Home Project 1999, 1)

Of the last 3 decades . . . No one disagrees on the problem: high concentrations of poor and poorly educated families in substandard housing—many on welfare and out of work—in an environment rife with crime, dysfunctional families, and domestic violence . . . The people who work with the inner city poor are attempting to get the message across that the greatest problem is not welfare, economics, or urban renewal, but the breakdown of morality and the historical foundations of family unity. (Center for Reclaiming America 1997, 1)

Again, black youth and households were represented as simple immigrants thrust into complex industrial cities. But now the dilemma was a people's cognitive rather than cultural simplicity. "These were kids and households," to Chicago Planner Devira Beverly (1991), "that often didn't understand the need for such city renewal. . . . Their ill-defined sense of community and city needs led to opposition and resistance." Here were struggling and confused people; basic civic duties often failed to register. And once relocated, in the view of Beverly and others, these people often recreated the community decline that made urban renewal a supposedly continuous stop-gap approach. Renewal forever chased decline that continuously popped up in correlation with black residency and black activity spaces. Black youth, a central element in this viewpoint, drew on pathologies in neighborhoods and housing projects and destructively downgraded much in their wake. As Philadelphia planner William Rafsky (1988) noted, "kids in these neighborhoods were a problem. They transported trouble and discord to schools, parks, streets, and downtown . . . that accelerated community and downtown decline."

By the late 1960s, the strong feelings many Americans had about cities had turned more ambivalent. As the above discussion reveals, cities in the common imagining had become more crazed and their raw social character more raw. They continued to be seen as the leading edge of America's industrial might, but were also viewed as sickly and ill. In much reporting, the problem was demographic and local in nature. Cities had become populated by new populations, particularly African Americans, that changed the culture, safety, and livability of cities. Once-small ghettos, enlarged and more decayed, had emerged as ominous futuristic elements.

Postwar Suburbanization and City Decline II, 1968–1980

Suburbanization and city decline after 1967 accelerated. U.S. suburbs gained over eighteen million people and more than three million jobs in the late 1960s and 1970s (Muller 2000). In the 1970s, U.S. cities experienced a population and tax base decline of 4 and 7 percent (*Time Almanac* 1990). The country's five largest cities, New York, Chicago, Los Angeles, Philadelphia, and Houston, lost over 965,000 people (Jakle and Wilson 1992). The most devastated city, Newark, lost nearly 100,000 people between 1970 and 1990 to shrink to 275,221 (*Time Almanac* 1990). Industrial and corporate exodus was even more extreme. In 1960 thirteen of the top twenty largest corporations in America were headquartered in U.S. cities; by 1970 four were here. Among the top corporate one hundred, twenty-three of the previous sixty-eight city-based corporations had relocated to suburbia by 1970.

This city decline received much attention in routine reportage in newspapers, magazines, essays, and TV (Beauregard 1993). But it was communicated most poignantly through a flow of media-chronicled extraordinary events that again blamed problem black kids and black communities. The first dominant event represented—the urban riots of the late 1960s, notably in Newark, Chicago, Gary, Los Angeles, Detroit, and Cleveland—seared the public psyche. The largest riot, in Detroit in 1967, which was reported on from coast to coast in stark terms, saw over eight hundred buildings pillaged and burned (James Q. Wilson 1970). Property damage was estimated at over $70 million (Glazer 1970). The second-worse riot, a weeklong affair in Los Angeles that received equally widespread and stark coverage, decimated Watts. In reportage, most buildings along the main avenue were destroyed or looted (Beauregard 1993). In all, 34 people were killed, 1,032 injured, 3,950 arrested, 600 buildings partially or totally destroyed, and $50 million in property damage incurred. By 1969, the U.S. media had provided detailed reporting on thirty-four cities that experienced urban riots (Beauregard 1993).

Reports of riots activated a sense that minorities had grown restless and volatile. In theme, once compliant and law-abiding minorities could now be easily seduced to purvey destruction. The presentation was ominous: Blacks and Hispanics now lurked and paced city streets in defiance of civility and order. These cities had become their turf, a place they controlled. Seizure of urban space was all but complete as a sea of ominous individuals colonized what had once been spaces of civility. A difficult-to-understand immigrant now dominated cities; tranquility and assimilation were becoming past things. The problem—their ways, values, temperaments—was something new and threatening for the future of cities. Three weeks after the Detroit riots, for example, *U.S. News and World Report* (1967a, 29; 1967b, 37) noted: "Anarchy has become a threat to all of America's cities, including the nation's capital . . . the fact that so many Americans do live apart from the crime-ridden and riot-plagued central cities in an atmosphere of law, order, and stability is seen as a reservoir of strength for the U.S."

As before, kids dominated city streets, scared away whites and investment, and deepened ghetto and downtown decline (Rafsky 1988). But now they and their families perversely compensated for inability to mainstream by going one step further, establishing their own social and moral worlds. A new black ghetto, one bearing a tangle of pathologies, had emerged. New ghetto norms now sanctioned and ritualized youth destructive acts that devastated black neighborhoods and downtowns. To Indianapolis councilman Bart Parenti (1984), "in the 1970s, once troubled but hesitant kids confidently strolled and marauded to proudly show and flaunt their identity." To Parenti, "these kids wanted to be seen and responded to . . . it was a new ghetto youth and they embraced a new way of seeing the world." A new ghetto social and moral reality had appeared: these kids were at the center of it.

The race riots ceased by the early 1970s but the public further recoiled from presentation of a new extraordinary city process: rising crime. Between 1970 and 1974, the nation's murder rate and robbery rate officially climbed 30 and 26 percent (Teaford 1990). Sensational reporting of city crime from coast to coast seared America: violent crime quickly became synonymous with cities and pulsating ghettos. This perception deepened the sense of city decline, allowing mayors like Ralph Perk of Cleveland, Peter Flaherty of Pittsburgh, and Abe Beam of New York City to obtain public office. These new defenders of authority, often ex-cops (Charles Stenvig of Minneapolis, Frank Rizzo of Philadelphia), boldly spoke about rising crime and need for stern order. They were the ones who shed their holsters to make a real difference. With their police backgrounds, they purportedly knew what order was and how it could be restored.

Detroit assumed the moniker of "Murder City" because of a steady stream of media-hyped homicides (see Lineberry and Sharkansky 1978). In Philadelphia, the media orchestrated a crime panic that spotlighted ex-cop Mayor Frank Rizzo promising a law-and-order campaign that "will make Attila the Hun look like a faggot." His goal, the media reported, was to attack "lenient judges" who repetitiously turn "wild animals" back on streets that polluted Philadelphia (in Teaford 1990). In Los Angeles, where getting tough on crime was extolled in the media, new get-tough street tactics followed. Police were given permission to deploy helicopters to maintain an average nineteen-hour-per-day vigil over "high crime areas" after 1970 that was tactically coordinated with patrol cars (see Davis 1990). To facilitate ground-air synchronization, thousands of residential rooftops were painted with street numbers to impose a massive surveillance pattern across the city.

At the same time, stories of New York City's 1975 fiscal crisis and its spread to other cities crystallized the sense of urban erosion. New York's play with fiscal default in the early 1970s was the public's initial glimpse (Buck and Fainstein 1992). Its full-blown fiscal default and bankruptcy captivated the public. New York City was offered as leader of a new, fiscally struggling city. Cities, particularly New York, were now barely working and strained to pay their bills. Now, many believed, New York and other cities fought to survive rather than to revive. They fought to thwart bankruptcy, outflow of capital, spread of housing abandonment, and job loss. As *Village Voice* reporter Ken Auletta and *New York Review of Books* writer Jason Epstein noted about New York:

> Federal aid [to New York] has dried up, years of fiscal gimmicks have sapped our credit, and optimistic slogans have served as a narcotic, inducing us to avoid the painful choices we and our leaders must begin to make. (Auletta 1975, 8)

> [T]he prevailing wisdom is that New York and the other older Eastern cities are finished anyway. The country's future has shifted westward . . . As New York once carelessly discarded its own marginal neighborhoods, so America may have decided that New York itself can now be junked. (Epstein 1976, 22)

Many prominent urbanists blamed African American youth and communities for these urban problems. To George Sternlieb (1970), cities in the 1970s had become full-fledged storehouses for residual people. They had evolved into playgrounds and gratification centers for those whom society could not productively mobilize. Sternlieb called these new cities "sandboxes" where the poor and socially maladjusted were systematically dumped. Norton Long (1971) similarly presented the city as akin to an Indian reservation with clients and keepers. In this kind of reservation, to Long, minority populations relied on transfer payments under the watchful eye of regulative state keepers. Moreover, William Baer in 1975 (in Teaford 1990) discussed cities as cemeteries. Given current demographics, to Baer, the death of cities is now coming to pass, even as it is "hindered by expertise, detoured by cajolery, impeded by charismatic leadership, and delayed by simple faith; but it will come."

But against this tide, government and capital continued efforts to recapture cities. They again trotted out reclamation rhetoric and new glittering programs like Urban Development Action Grants, Urban Homesteading, and Block Grants. These programs were the 1970s instruments of supposed progressive change (see Browsher 1980; Glickman 1980). Republicans held the reins of power in Washington and advertised a new kind of discipline—solid and sensible Republican ventures steeped in the New Federalism—to economically and civically renew cities. To Richard Nixon (1969), "[i]n rebuilding our cities . . . we must press urgently forward . . . With the new Federalism . . . we will make a crucial breakthrough toward better [living] . . . in our towns and in our cities across America." This optimistic Republican posturing was the latest pro-recapture rhetoric. Idealistic Democrats and naïve enthusiasts of urban renewal had failed, Republicans said, but their inspired interventions could renew cities.

But this government response failed to stem economic and physical decline, and black kids and communities again were blamed. A leading indicator of failure was the 1970s unprecedented wave of housing abandonment (see Dear 1976; Van Allsberg 1975). Slum clearance and neighborhood conservation measures funded under new Republican initiatives rarely halted blight that contagiously spread across downtowns. In 1975, there were an estimated 199,000 abandoned housing units in New York City, 44,500 in Chicago, 62,000 in Detroit, 33,000 in Philadelphia, and 30,000 in St. Louis (Salins 1980). More than 1.1 million home-owned and 1.5 million rental units were removed from the national housing market in the 1970s. By the late 1970s, large portions of New York's South Bronx lay in ruins, entire blocks burned out and abandoned (see Bromley 1997). Flanking struggling central business districts, they gave the media and public one more visible urban ill to ponder.

Fingering black kids, families, and communities continued in the context of the media's providing stepped-up, graphic reportage of a renewed symbol of urban distress: decimated ghettos and downtowns. Mid-1970s exposés on ripped-up ghettos in Cleveland (Hough), New York (Harlem, Bedford Stuyvesant), Chicago (South Side), Philadelphia (North Philly), and most U.S. cities introduced a new presence—drugs—that post-1980 representations were to dramatically embellish. Now, drugs (cocaine, dope, heroin) had found their way into the ghetto and accelerated youth deviance. Drug houses, drug-selling gangs, and stoned-out youth appeared in growing numbers to hasten community and city decline. Kids could not seem to resist drugs; others fashioned perverse lives by selling it. In this reporting, drug-infused ghettos were provided the kids, values, and lifestyles that allowed a seamless presentation of "crack-cocaine-destroyed neighborhoods" in the 1980s. As the *Chicago Tribune* noted: "On the South Side . . . it's the dope fiends . . . The big problem is . . . the threat of youth gangs in black areas . . . [Many are] afraid of [such] criminals. [Many are] afraid to walk home alone at night" (1978, 1).

Invention of a monolithic black youth, the troubled compensatory kid (labeled "underclass kids" in the 1980s), now assumed center stage. These were tragic but ghastly figures, kids either falling into aberrant and destructive "drug" or "crime" worlds or born into these worlds. In both cases, their norms and customs attacked and eroded communities and cities. Hardened poverty and pathological culture that gripped these kids predisposed them to drugs, crime, vice, and urban destruction. In the context of frequently stark and "factual" presentations, fears and anxieties were collapsed into a trusty urban folk-villain who became a simple explanation of ghetto realities. Elijah Anderson, in *Streetwise,* describes the new black youth:

> [He] has a "string" of women. He may feel little obligation toward them and the children he has fathered, but on "mothers day," when welfare checks come to these single mothers, his self-aggrandizement consumes his whole being as he attempts to impress people through displays of material success like expensive clothes and family cars. Eagerly awaiting his message are the unemployed young black men, demoralized by what they see as a hopeless financial situation and inclined to emulate his style and values. For some who follow this model, great though often fleeting financial success may be in store. More often a trail of unfulfilled dreams, broken lives, jail, and even death awaits. (Anderson 1993, 3–4)

The Latest Narcotic

Across America attempts at city recapture persisted in the late 1970s. With the sense of much at stake, capital and America initiated another scheme: gentrification. I suggest that this can be seen as capital's latest strategy to restore the city's accumulation function and symbolic significance. Cities were still staging grounds for production and symbols of U.S. capitalist virility in the late 1970s; desire to reclaim their past economic clout and glory persisted. To Christine Boyer (1983), landscapes that are powerful economic engines and key symbols in a cultivated national psyche do not easily go away. Even as they wither, according to Boyer, many will desire their restoration and rejuvenation.

As in previous strategies, the media led the charge. After years of abandonment, to the media urban turnaround seemed possible. Disenfranchised suburbanites and investors were rediscovering cities (see Smith and Williams 1986; Knopp and Kujawa 1993), and a new cast of urban salvationists was displayed: heroic gentrifiers, entrepreneurial developers, bold investors, and opportunistic city governments. These were the people that could make a difference and restore the greatness of cities. *Time's* 1981 cover that featured a picture of James Rouse and the statement "Cities Are Fun" personified this new media offering. Now, in rhetoric, possibility existed to reverse urban ills and recapture cities for people who deserved them. But to these enthusiasts, courage, conviction, and uncompromising confrontation with the enemy (blight, destructive culture, harmful neighborhoods) were necessary.

The tale has been widely chronicled: courageous conquerors tirelessly taming the wilds of a barren inner city frontier (see Smith 1996). Spurred by what was right, cities would be reclaimed by the adventurous and socially responsible. Sweat equity, boundless energy, and uncompromising confrontation with blight were the keys. These public emissaries would transform cities into what they once supposedly were: viable workspaces, interesting playscapes, and vibrant consumption places. In the process, black slums and ghettos would be replaced by the light of civilized communities. Neighborhoods devoid of life would be filled with living and community commitment. The assets of gentrifiers, to Indianapolis Planning Head B. Call (1987), were "their hands, their hearts, their brains." Call believed that "[t]heir skills and lifestyles" would "renew cities that had fallen on hard times."

At the core of this tale was a key figure, the gentrifier icon, whose conservative values ultimately made it acceptable as an ideal type. Superficially, gentrifiers were said to reject the aesthetic of suburbs in favor of a more freewheeling ambience. Instantaneous consumption, conspicuous display of historicity, architectural distinctiveness, and breakdown of overt racial and class antipathies were their progressive ideals. But they were crafted to retain the suburb's deep patriarchal conservatism: commitment to segmented socioeconomic spaces, racially partitioned cities, the dominant community-controlling gaze of the wealthy, orientation to traditional monogamous sexualities (gay gentrified neighborhoods excluded), and belief in cultural conquest of ghetto and urban space. Bearing this conservatism, these people could be comfortably extolled as leaders in a city revitalization movement.

It follows that sense of citizenship in gentrification pronouncement was not extended to everyone, particularly black youth and their communities. African Americans were brutally coded into oblivion. Gentrification was all about supplanting a supposed underclass culture and spaces and destroying any sense of lower-class living. In aspiration, the decades-long ordeal of dysfunctional families and kids populating inner cities could be eradicated. To *American Enterprise Online* writer Andres Duany (2001), "Gentrification is . . . good news, for there is nothing more unhealthy for a city than a monoculture of poverty." Paraphrasing a police officer, Duany noted "urban problems are caused not by poverty, but a concentration of poverty . . ." What is sacrificed here, to Duany, is "decrepit area[s]," "ratty bad-food joints," and the "urban cycle of decay."

But amid the rhetoric, the reality of America's 1970s downtowns soon set in. Most poignantly, gentrification proved to be a small-scale process that barely bumped against the still strong tide of urban decline (see Bourne 1993, 1996). In most cities, only a handful of neighborhoods and districts gentrified (New York City's Manhattan experience is the most obvious exception). For every neighborhood and commercial block gentrified, many others decayed and struggled. This process, contrary to the suggestions of boosters and prognosticators, was not a long-term reversal of migration and capital investment. In form, gentrification tended to express itself as tiny enclaves of middle-income and upper-middle-income residency with nearby support retailing (Bourne 1993). And many gentrifiers were not disillusioned suburbanites but long-term urban dwellers who came together to agglomerate in urban space. Gentrification as back-to-the-city, like many of its supposed features, was a myth of the media, of chambers of commerce, and of real-estate capital.

The reality of the late 1970s U.S. city was limited opportunities for "hyper-accumulation" in many urban real-estate markets and immense difficulty in restoring a national icon. The media has been, not surprisingly, slow to acknowledge this limitation. Among those that have, the tendency has been to blame black communities and youth one more time. These things again widely assumed the role of mobile and intransigent problems that blunted upgrading. Their supposed behaviors and practices—high rates of crime, devaluing land, destroying property and hopes for community renewal—have been supposed plagues to long-term stable investment and middle-class relocation. As HUD Secretary Henry Cisneros noted, "Tearing down [ghetto] housing and replacing it in inner cities [private-market upgrading] is like bailing water out of the boat while at the other end someone's got a hose and they're filling it from the ocean [perpetuating disinvestment] . . . No matter how fast you bail, you can't beat the water coming in." Cisneros offered "hope against hope—I hope against reason—that the other things we're doing will keep us even" (in Deparle 1996, 15).

The Context of Republican Politics

This chapter has discussed dominant postwar representations of urban black youth and communities as historical context for the rise of post-1980 "black-on-black violence" discourse. Against this evolving stream of representations, this post-1980 discourse arose. As discourses have always done, they drew on prevailing meanings and understandings to provide an updated, contemporary reality. But there is another contextual dimension to this discourse rise that must be briefly discussed: the emergence of Reagan conservatism after 1980. This dimension is important: "black-on-black violence" understandings were constituted in this immediate political climate. This became, post-1980, Sarah Diamond's (1995) setting of political and moral normalcy. In this political setting, social and moral norms were established, politicians sought support and re-election, legislation was passed, and social issues like "black-on-black violence" constructed.

Post-1980 politics in America are best understand by initially referencing late 1970s conditions. In the late 1970s, America seemed a nation in transition. As now widely chronicled, a sense of failing cities, faltering regions, declining international standing, strangulating inflation, and stagnant material conditions haunted mainstream thought (see Steinfels 1979; Diamond 1995). The dynasty and well-being of America seemed unstable. "From the vantage-point of the lazy and sedate 1990s," according to Champaign, Illinois, mayor Dan McCollum (1995), "it is hard to imagine the reality of this time [late 1970s and early 1980s]. It was a time of worry and concern for the state of society, the nation, one's future." Economics, politics, and material well-being seemed up in the air, a new world and a new America seemed on the verge. Commentators identified this malaise as "the new cynicism, "the new jaded America," the "angry

America" that demarcated a troubled public (see *U.S. News and World Report* 1975; *Business Week* 1979).

In the whirl of competitive politics, conservative Republicans seized the moment. They deftly played to American anxieties to offer simple solutions and villains to American problems. Hyperaggressive politicians and commentators peddled an attractive America rooted in nativist delusion, ethnocentric provocation, and imperialist appeal. Creation of villains, domestic and international, featured "inner city blacks," "Caribbean immigrants," "Asian investors," "Cuban boat people," "welfare mothers," and "black families." These villains, rooted in commonsense understandings (that is, a history of villainizing), resonated in this troubled period. This making of villains thus reproduced past discourses that these immigrants, racial minorities, and entrepreneurs were national problems (see Schneider 1988; Laws 1997).

This oratory bolstered by conservative money and influence saturated America. The late 1970s growth in number and size of conservative think-tanks was critical. By 1980 this number included Alliance for America, American Conservative Union, American Family Association, American Renewal Project, Christian Coalition, Citizens for Law and Order, Citizens for a Sound Economy, Coalitions for America, Concerned Women for America, Council for Citizens Against Government Waste, Eagle Forum, Empower America, and the Empowerment Network (I list only national organizations from *A* to *E*). The most prominent, the American Enterprise Institute, Heritage Foundation, Hudson Institute, and Cato Institute, spent over $10 million to produce research and affect public policy between 1978 and 1982 (House Democratic Policy Committee 1996). This was an increase of more than 46 percent from the previous four years (see House Democratic Policy Committee 1996).

This aggressiveness continued in the 1980s and 1990s. Between 1992 and 1994, twelve conservative foundations provided over $210 million to fund production and dissemination of conservative ideas (National Committee for Responsive Philanthropy 1997). Over $80 million went to organizations pushing unregulated "free markets" and undermining social programs and government regulations. The leading recipient, the Heritage

Foundation, received nearly $9 million; the American Enterprise and Cato Institutes received nearly as much. The other $130 million went to magazine and media pressure groups, cable networks, and TV programs. This pattern of expenditure dwarfed liberal foundation gift-giving. To Sally Covington, director of the National Committee on Responsive Philanthropy (NCRP), "the role that conservative foundations played in reinvigorating the institutional base of American conservatism simply ha[d] no parallel in the liberal funding community" (National Committee for Responsive Philanthropy 1997).

But this was only the beginning. At the same time, an ascendant group of "candid" spokespeople battered America with a spicy diet of conservative rhetoric. Rush Limbaugh, a failed salesperson and radio disc jockey in six states, became an overnight media sensation. His radio show could be heard on over one hundred radio stations daily by 1990. William Bennett, President Reagan's Department of Education secretary and President George H. W. Bush's "drug czar," was equally vocal, castigating deviants from conservatism in talk shows, newspaper columns, media press releases, and magazine narrations. Conservative broadcaster Paul Harvey, a high school dropout from Salinas, Kansas, daily spouted reactionary diatribes on over ninety syndicated radio stations. Conservative columnists Robert Novak, William Buckley, Mona Charen, Linda Chavez, Dr. Edwin J. Feulner Jr., Alan Keyes, James Kilpatrick, Charles Krauthammer, John Leo, A. M. Rosenthal, William Safire, Joseph Sobron, Cal Thomas, Emmett Tyrell Jr., Ben Wattenberg, George Will, and Walter Williams also barraged the public with conservative editorials and opinions.

These commentators played to and made comforting realities. They played to fears, nurtured the sense of easy villains, and projected a glittery national trajectory. America was spoon-fed simple causes for problems and fears, a virtuous national identity, ludicrously simple villains, and deceptively easy solutions to affairs. Like Sartre's being searching for the orderly ground that infuses sense of self and purpose, America found it in this combination. Conservatives, in other words, were not beneath pandering to anything to shape American thought. While Jimmy Carter spoke of the difficulties in a new world order, Ronald Reagan articulated the new morning in America. We had struggled with moral consciousness and prevailed, candidate Reagan said; now it was springtime in America. Before us lay opportunities to perpetuate what we always knew we were, the dominant power broker across the globe.

It is of course too simplistic to reduce America's post-1980 conservative turn to Marx's "sack of potatoes" phenomenon (*The Eighteenth Brumaire of Louis Napoleon*). Here populations simply follow the dictates of dominant ideology regardless of its content and ingenuity. In contrast, conservatives deftly took charge and exploited a vulnerable time in American thought. Their expansive energies, coercive ideas, devastating appeals, and richly illuminating metaphors left their competition groping. Conservative politics post-1980 were an ongoing human accomplishment. They not merely beat progressives to the punch, they effectively punched progressives out.

At the center of this situation was the resonance of Ronald Reagan. Like few before him, Reagan plundered America's fears and anxieties to sustain a reality suiting America's darkest needs. Reagan was the central figure that for the moment ameliorated turmoil. Turning America inward to find redemption, he offered elaborate celebratory rhetoric about American economic and cultural superiority. To Reagan, Americans had been self-critical too long, had dwelled in a groundless self-doubt. We were still leader of the free world, Reagan asserted repeatedly, and nothing had changed. "It's morning in America," he incessantly declared, and what we once were we would continue to be. Reagan deftly articulated a distinction between rhetoric and reality that Americans easily understood. Feelings of a country in decline, he said, were a fairy tale. Offering this view, he proclaimed, were cynics, liberals, "politicized" Democrats, disillusioned leftists who dwelled in pessimism and fantasy. Reagan's reality was a milieu of continued American power and clout. It was no coincidence America was still the world's most feared and envied nation, Reagan said, and things were only going to get better.

To Reagan, we had good reason to feel good about ourselves. His initiatives were a beacon of light to guide Americans through the uncertainties of a complex late-twentieth-century global world. His populism cut through political confusion and complexity to identify simple good, bad, right, wrong, correct, and incorrect. This message massaged and built up a fragile American psyche. At a time national sense of self and dominance seemed to be waning, Reagan challenged this outlook. Amid a world of growing complexity, Reagan gave us simplicity. At a time when problems seemed to be multiplying and having confusing causes, Reagan provided easy evils and villains. Our biggest problem, Reagan skillfully pointed out, was ourselves: our confidence, will, and desire to strike out on behalf of America and to retain our hegemonic role.

Reagan anchored his rhetoric in a mythical version of American history that was the "field of understanding" for others to articulate the conservative view of "black-on-black violence." A new "power to the people," a core populist outcry, was at the center of this version of history. America, to Reagan, had been built piece by piece into the most powerful nation on the earth by unhinging the will and expertise of people. A "private" America, allowed to express itself unhampered by government or welfare-dependent populations, flexed its muscles to build this powerful nation. The only "special interest" group that deserved insider access to wealth and power, according to Reagan, was the special interest group called America. To Reagan:

> We hear much of special interest groups. Well, our concern must be for a special interest group that has been too long neglected. It knows no sectional boundaries or ethnic and racial divisions, and it crosses no political party lines. It is made up of men and women who raise our food, patrol our streets, man our mines and factories, teach our children, keep our homes, and heal us when we're sick—professionals, industrialists, shopkeepers, clerks, cabbies, truck drivers. They are, in short, "We the people," this breed called Americans. (1981)

But Reagan doled out more hatred than he cared to admit. As part of this field of understanding, Reagan talked at length about the urban poor, dividing them into three types: cheats who defraud taxpayers, addicted welfare recipients trapped in dependency on the system, and truly needy, disabled people (Weiler and Pearce 1992). The third type, supposedly a small minority of poor people, was the sole group society should help. The other two were professional poverty recipients who sought to avoid honest labor. "Virtually every American who shops in a supermarket is aware of the daily abuses that take place in the food stamp program—which has grown 16,000 percent in the last 16 years," Reagan noted (1982). Reagan's fraudulent poor, strong in mind and body, used the politics of racism and discrimination to rationalize perverse plunder. Addicted welfare recipients, more well-meaning in possibly having some sense of civic responsibility, had their moral fiber destroyed by debilitating welfare programs.

In this context, Reagan marshaled a public hostility to "welfare people," "Welfare Queens," "Welfare Kings," "the malignancy of welfarism," "criers of racism," and "the pretending disadvantaged" (see Weiler and Pearce 1992). The American dream, to Reagan, "is denied to no one, each individual has the right to fly as high as his strength and ability will take him" (1982). Notions of racism, educational limitations, and economic restrictions were mere constructions to exploit generosity. America, to Reagan, was at war with not only relativist lifestyles, hedonist values, alternative sexualities, atheists, and agnostic sensibilities, but with welfarist propagators. This was the mobile army of cheats who defiled neighborhoods, created surges in nonmarital births, filled local homeless shelters, overpopulated public spaces, aggressively panhandled on the streets, and eroded public spaces.

At the head of the pack was the proud and defiant Welfare Queen. She had oodles of kids and welfare boyfriends, scorned mainstream values, and hustled and plundered for sport. Like the ubiquitous strong and taut black male whose food stamps bought T-bone steaks and potato chips, she laughed at a system that was keenly manipulated. Place of occupancy, "black inner cities," was saturated with pathology. It was the home for hustle, shake and bake, cheaters, people taunting the system, and kids drinking up vile values. In the images of Reagan, a concerned world peered with abhorrence at this spectacle of dysfunction.

With this rhetoric, Reagan effectively demonized the poor and substantially shrunk poverty programs. Now only the "truly needy" deserved public support, that is, those who could not work and lacked other means of support. The Omnibus Budget Reconciliation Act (OBRA) of 1981 removed from eligibility approximately 50 percent of the 450,000 to

500,000 Aid to Families with Dependent Children (AFDC) recipients (Levitan 1985). Another 40 percent of working AFDC recipients lost portions of their benefits (Levitan 1985). An OBRA provision also authorized states to operate work relief programs, what Reagan called workforce. This work for benefits was reinforced in the Tax Equity and Fiscal Responsibility Act of 1982, which required recipients to seek employment before receiving welfare benefits. Levitan (1985) estimates that OBRA changes in AFDC pushed 600,000 people below the poverty line in 1982 alone without considering impacts of that year's national recession.

Reagan did not champion government involvement in cities. Urban policy was all but forgotten that less communicated the expendability of cities than the expendability of "welfarist government" in all places and circumstances. Reagan was astute enough to realize the public cared about cities. This was one of the "national treasures" he frequently spoke of. But he persuasively argued that cities could be revitalized by turning them over to private-sector forces and processes. His lack of "traditional" urban programs, he proclaimed, would be best for cities. His sole urban policy initiative, the urban enterprise zone, conformed to this rhetoric of nurturing the private sector (Burnier and Descuter 1992). In the end, Reagan and Congress slashed the Housing and Urban Development budget from $36 billion in 1980 to $18 billion in 1987 (Burnier and Descuter 1992).

This discussion of Reagan's presentation of society, cities, welfare queens, footloose black men, and subcultures is important to this study. Through these presentations, conservatives confidently chronicled "truths" about "black-on-black violence." This violence vision, we will learn in chapters 3 and 4, depended upon establishing a cast of villains, victims, and ominous forces to situate notions of cause. Reagan's notion of society, cities, black subculture, and the others stood in for this purpose. These established "stocks of understanding" were ripe for being tapped: they were resonant and could help current political projects. This "black-on-black vision" depended upon them to give it form and meaning. Without this understanding, there could have been no "black-on-black violence" vision. In this violence discourse, the past and present seamlessly meshed.

PART TWO

◢ ◢ ◢

The Discourses

3

The Conservative Discourse

The General Gaze

After 1980, diverse conservatives (for example, national essayists, city editorialists, community commentators) spoke widely about "black-on-black violence." To advance a coherent vision, inner city social life was discussed from changing visual perspectives. These narrativists, conscious of the relation of sight to power, most fundamentally staked out a "ground-level" position to advance the discourse. This grassroots eye captured disorder and dysfunction in streets, corners, shops, parks, and schools. Finest appearances—looks, strolls, acts, body movements—were made meaning-laden and significant. This grassroots eye zipped in and out of streets and blocks and magnified what other observers and interpreters supposedly missed. Raced and classed people were made to "reveal" true essences in the most simple acts. With this gaze, no indicator of social disorganization could elude the roving conservative eye.

But in the next instant position shifted to the "top of the territory" to demonstrate the magnitude of the problem. This expansive gaze glimpsed across cities and metropolitan areas in an all-encompassing view. These narrativists situated themselves like de Certeau's (1994) gaze atop the Empire State Building to see in and across vast landscapes. Cities and regions, from this vantage point, were reduced to specks of easily visualized dots confidently read and chronicled. These conservatives, like magicians, glided across vast spaces to discuss multiple common villains (black youth, black families, black culture) and salvationists (themselves, conservative policy leaders) in this violence. Spaces and agglomerations of human bodies, in a seizure and appropriation, became passive things to narrate.

But the conservative discourse offered this bold "truth-telling" in the context of also striving for acceptance. Like any discourse, it desired to gain support in the frame of speaking its truths. To gain acceptance, conservatives made themselves intellectual interrogators that destroyed myths and hewed new paths for understanding. They purportedly subjected social conventions to the cold eye of reason that differentiated them from other chroniclers of the world. They proclaimed themselves uncompromisingly objective and absolute tellers of truth. Someone supposedly had to step forward to unearth truths about this violence; they were willing. Lures that supposedly contaminated other narrativists—petty politics, greed, ambition—were shunned by them. In this context, their rendition of this violence fingered "black culture" and "black youth."

Two kinds of presentations characterized the discourse: the critical "black-on-black violence" essay and the no-holds-barred reporting of community decline (with "black-on-black violence" at its center). Reporting of community decline, first, offered straightforward and bold truth-telling. Conservatives positioned themselves as courageous and clear observers who entered unsavory ghettos and went public with findings. This reportage provided blunt but colorful images of declining kids and places: drug sellers on street corners, marauding gangs, decrepit social conditions, lost families, and failing social institutions. Metaphors of armies, wars, military operations, alien worlds, and brazen youth populated images. In theme, once-stable social environments had fallen on ghastly times; these places were now decimated. *Chicago Tribune Magazine* writer Paul Weingarten provides a vivid example:

> When the sun sets on Chicago's West Side, the armies of the night come out to play. People in the neighborhoods retreat into their homes—or if they're brave, to their porches—and wait. Out in the night, a new order takes shape. It is an alien world, strange and incomprehensible. A world where junior-high kids carry shotguns, and no one ventures out unarmed.
>
> Street gangs control the night. The gangs have a mission here, a sense of purpose and honor . . . and vengeance. The code of this West is shoot to kill. They don't care who's in the way.

Gang banging is what they call this game. It is not the common reference to gang rape; rather, it means anything from roaming the streets splattering graffiti everywhere to snuffing a rival gang member. In many ways it is a game, a grisly version of King of the Mountain where gangs jostle for position by "rolling on each other—stabbing or shooting—then girding against retaliation. In these neighborhoods, the kids start playing the game when they're 8 or 10. They stop when they move, go to jail, or die.

Many of the neighborhoods look like the results of something close to a scorched-earth policy. Amid dilapidated apartments and crumbling homes stand empty lots full of rubble, weeds, broken glass, and the rusting hulks of stripped cars. Windows everywhere are boarded up. The only fresh paint is gang graffiti.

If the leaders are smart and ruthless, the gang rises, and people get hurt. When the leaders go to jail, the gang usually falls apart. "The black gangs disappeared in the early seventies," says Deputy Superintendent Joseph McCarthy, who is in charge of the entire Gang Crimes Operation. "Now they've re-emerged as the leaders have come out of jail." (Weingarten 1982, 1)

The penetrating "black-on-black violence" essay, similarly, gave the appearance of cutting through political correctness and grimy ghettos to reveal truth. More so than the no-holds-barred reporting, it dwelled on this violence's supposed root problems and causes. It tended to be less image-rich and metaphorically evocative, but also invoked pathological ghettos seared by drug addiction, moral decay, social disorganization, imploding culture, and irresponsible black youth. An editorial, "The Black Underclass," by *U.S. News and World Report* chairman and editor-in-chief Mortimer B. Zuckerman, illustrates. He writes:

In Harlem, a controversy arises over two brothers, young blacks, accused by a policeman of harassing him. In a scuffle, one of the brothers, Edmund Perry, is fatally shot. He turns out to be not just a street tough but a graduate of a famous prep school, with a scholarship to Stanford. In Chicago, Benjy Wilson, a high-school basketball star, is shot by two teenage gang members. There is a common thread and a common but long-concealed dilemma. Perry and Wilson and Wilson's murderers were all from families abandoned by the fathers. And Wilson himself had just fathered a child out of wedlock.

The dilemma is this: Why is it that two decades of visible black progress, with billions spent in welfare and training, have also seen the explosive rise of an alienated black underclass whose rootlessness, violence and debased values dominate the ghetto? Three causes have been argued: unemployment, welfare dependency and the feminization of poverty. They do not adequately explain what is happening. Many statistics of social anarchy apply to the poor regardless of race. A way of life utterly separate from the American mainstream has become associated with poor city blacks more than any other group. One stunning statistic illuminates the catastrophe—approximately 80 percent of all black children in the ghettos are born out of wedlock.

The truth is we are up against the limits of public policy. At the heart of the disaster there is a vacuum of values. In the ghettos across America, too many young black men roam the streets and too many young black mothers struggle alone to raise another generation of fatherless black youth for reform to come about via a traditional politics and programs . . . The hardest job is cultural; to arrest the moral deterioration occurring in the poorest segments of black culture and to reverse it . . . White institutions cannot [do this] . . . Only blacks can. . . . What is at stake are millions of lives and the long-term health of our cities as centers of commerce and culture. (Zuckerman 1986, 17)

Both of these statements were supposedly straightforward and blunt renditions of African American kids and neighborhoods (Thomas Sowell's [1984] no-holds-barred truths about black youth in ghettos). But this chapter chronicles that this offering was much more nuanced and creative. To reveal this complexity, I focus on the "fields of understanding" that anchored these blunt assertions. Beneath seemingly simple and straightforward declarations of dysfunctional kids in destructive culture, I suggest, were complex constructions of reality that functioned to normalize these assertions. This "bedrock" of meanings placed in people, places, and processes framed presentations of black-on-black violence. It drew together diverse elements and objects, laced them with coherent meanings, and blended them to "platform" discussions of this violence. This said, I begin my excavation.

The Cast of Villains

Exploding onto the scene in the early 1980s, the conservative discourse offered a host of villains involved in this violence. It played to established stereotypes and understandings to illuminate them: black families, black inner city youth, and liberal black politicians. These constructions gained meaning in a melodrama filled with caricatured people, extreme social and emotive states, incessant action, and constant confrontations between virtue and vice. In this context, villains carried the dilemmas of race, class, and space: the influence of blackness, ghetto life, and inner city space. "Black-on-black violence," in this sense, would not be known by nuanced inspection but by elaborate codification. This violence, widely chronicled and discussed, would stay a one-dimensional performance of inner city poor minorities. With this narrative strategy, people could easily grasp the issue's real story by knowing the codes.

Inner City Black Youth

The central villain made and displayed in the discourse was "black inner city youth." This elaborate but caricatured presentation was built around a central dilemma, cultural dysfunctionalism. These kids, as in previous renditions (see chapter 2), struggled to subsist in complex and sprawling cities. Simple beings thrust into socially complicated cities created turmoil, and, not surprisingly, much violence. The result changed black inner cities, exacerbated things with its litany of horrendous, ensnaring presences. Ghetto deterioration physically and socially powerfully imprinted this youth's consciousness and behavior. These generic kids had all but ceased attempts to integrate into city social life: ghetto worlds now preoccupied them. Past conservative successes in ravaging these kids in discourses, not to mention the dawn of the Reagan 1980s, paved the way to embellish this villain.

Discussions had these kids prone to seamlessly assimilating underclass life. They were "blank-slate" beings drawn to an open and rough street. The lures of play and immediate gratification (street-corner bantering, selling drugs, "malling," walking the streets) intoxicated them. The street became their emotive home as they spurned school, work, and home. Indianapolis mayoral candidate Carl Moldthan (1987), vocal on "black-on-black violence," noted: "These kids acquired meaning in a daily round of "meeting up with other kids," "walk[ing] up and down streets at night," "losing themselves in worlds of hedonism and ritualized confrontation." The pull of the streets, in conservative narration, seemed beyond resistance. As *Chicago Sun-Times* writer Rick Soll noted in one youth's situation in Chicago:

> "I need some peace," he said, "to figure out all this craziness. So I can figure out a way around it. Could be, you know, I'm already trapped, still stuck, you know, on the damn South Side. Lookin' back, maybe I been trapped since the very damn day I stared messin' round with this s—." "Damn South Side," he said, "Got me when I was 13." But it got him before that. The South Side and the circumstances of despair it breeds were at him before he was born. It was then as it still is, a landscape of old death and fresh troubles, and it got him the day his old man got drunk and ditched a pregnant wife. (Soll 1985, 7)

But construction of the general black youth identity was complex and relied upon Lefebvre's narrated spaces in multiple ways. Conservatives, first, displayed a luminous space, "culturally infected inner city space," that reduced black-on-black assailants and black youth to common problem beings. Space is, to Lefebvre (1984), a medium waiting to be colonized as an identity-making resource; this is what conservatives did. All kids in the black inner city, placed in and made to harbor this space, became behaviorally and attitudinally similar. Discussions distinguished between "young thugs" and non-criminal black youth: Only one offered violence. But both were purportedly afflicted by infectious inner cities and in different ways (overt criminal activity, beliefs and attitudes about authority and society) opposed society. In the haze of projected stereotype, one acted out antisocietal impulses, the other harbored them. This generic kid, in violent or nonviolent states, ritually transgressed in either deed or thought.

This space, a staged place of unending horror, was populated with the most garish manifestations of social dysfunction: drug dealers, struggling families, unsafe streets, vile parks and open spaces, roaming gangs, and discordant kids. Dysfunctional values across this space could be seen in kids' looks, the elderly's careful walks, crumbling housing, gang forays across neighborhoods, and drug sales on street corners. The *Chicago Sun-Times* (1981b), for example, had this space "the new social . . . [with] stark, forbidding lots around . . . projects . . . [with] bleak eyesores and fallow ground [everywhere]. The *Chicago Tribune* (1994, 4) has this space "[filled with] gun-toting pimps and pushers who have turned their neighborhoods into war zones." This space, to the *Tribune* and the *Sun-Times,* reflected and transmitted pathologies in routine and ritual.

This space was an ideal identity-reductionist resource. Common thought views communities as transparent and revealing. In this setting, common thought connects community environment with human behavior. Neighborhood and people, in a dominant strand of belief, are intimately interwoven. The character and content assigned to neighborhood space thus make it an ideal person-making thing. In this context, conservatives placed vile and infectious values in a resonant inner city space that made visible an ambiguous destructive culture. In clear images, a process decimating kids could be "seen" and pointed to. Sight became the assertion's irrefutable proof, its actual reality. What inner city black kids had purportedly become, this transparent space displayed. In this way, space helped make a social process to understand all inner city black kids.

This youth construction was deepened by marking bodies in narratives, local reporters and columnists taking the lead. In seemingly objective reportage, supposed ills of inner cities powerfully appeared on bodies for all to read: faces, eyes, legs, looks, mode of dress. For popular consumption was the influence of a perverse space on "a kid." This discourse maneuver, according to bell hooks (1993), makes bodies a poignant text. Bodies are constantly read in the informal and formal of everyday life whose politics are typically taken for granted and infrequently challenged. This marking, to hooks, makes bodies "speak against themselves" as an index of their identity. Such coding communicates the "undeniable" realities of inner city black youth that go beyond language and formal communication.

These conservatives, most notoriously, widely coded the looks of inner city kids as dulled and primitive. Given the power to look, these kids peered but barely comprehended. For example, St. Louis politician Rik Mallory (1991), notorious for his renditions of "visual" black youth, describes these kids as "continuously eyeing . . . superficial things . . . and pace[ing] back and forth. They not only crowd street corners and look for things to do," according to Mallory, "they scowl at passers-by and become a source of community intimidation." At the core of Mallory's dysfunctional kids are defective visions. They needed to be taught to see: a racial and class space blinded them. Their eyes were, in the hands of Mallory, points of capture and coding in a "political anatomy" that powerfully condensed the conservative will.

Marking bodies also featured kids made to scowl at external intruders. The act was deft: to Diane Dubose Brunner (1999), the act of scowling communicates discordant and angry people. Its narrating reduces personalities to narrow temperaments and problem beings. Renditions of Indianapolis inner city life from conservative councilman Ben West (1987) were illustrative. West's inner city had "hardened street corner posses . . . glaring confrontationally at anyone in their path. . . . clusters of youth on street corners . . . eyeing all that moved." These kids, to West, "looked menacingly at outsiders with disdain, anger, and loathing." West's kids resented being read: facial expressions signaled a ritualized anger with "outsiders." Visual aggression showed a disdain for being objectively assessed: the light of truth about themselves had to be deflected. This way, these kids were set up to reject the most elementary act of human civility, simple observation. They were unable to stand simple contact with "outsiders" that communicated a central conservative theme: an immersion in a cultural wilderness.

Mouths of kids were also scripted to indicate this spatially infected youth. A confused and primitive speaking youth was frequently displayed. This ploy too was time-tested: to Eric Cheyfitz (1981), conservative racial ideology commonly communicates the unattainability of full humanity without eloquence and acceptable thought. Offering ignorance with conspicuously bad language displays part beast, a kind of monster. *Commentary* magazine's Midge Dector (1992, 21) notoriously illuminated this in an interview with the 8-Trey Gangster Crips (the group that supposedly sparked the 1992 Los Angeles riots). She writes: "When Koppel asked the boys about the white truck driver who had in full view of the nation been pulled from his truck and beaten, one of them replied, 'He knew better. He saw what was happening.' Said a second, 'It was a CIA.' A third pointed out, 'They saying that, well, we burning down our own community. I mean, we don't own none of these liquor stores.' " As Dector recounts, "one named Time Bomb was surprised that Koppel had never heard of him, 'Because of my background and my . . . years in prison for shooting, breaking and entering, and attempted murder.' "

This conservative seizure and scripting of African American youth bodies is anything but surprising. Such renderings of bodies, according to Tommy Lott (1999), have a long history in the United States. Many narrativists, in the era of slavery, focused on generic physique (huge brutish people), in the early twentieth century on nimble, lithe bodies (minstrelsy), in the middle twentieth century on fluid body parts (mobile urban people). Black bodies, in the words of Cameron McCarthy (1995), have continuously been used as potent semiotic cargo. Post-1980 conservatives continued this process but more profoundly tied bodies to ghetto space. Ghettos were the established incendiary places of dramatic economic and cultural transformation; their use was adroit. In this scripting, these kids could offer all manner of excuse about their role in this violence; the "truth" of culture and space on them was revealed in their talk, movement, and appearance.

Conservatives also widely revealed another key space, "deadly gang space," to communicate the new black youth. This space, relentlessly narrated and packed with meaning, displayed the scariest extreme of the recent racial and cultural fall. It, banishing any evidence of calmness and civility, displayed inner cities colonized by horrific and territorial gangs. These groups of kids were typically immersed in drug-dealing and sought to control turf and to intimidate. Where there was once some normalcy, now there were only brute youth and struggle for terrain. More bluntly than any representation of inner city in the discourse, black youth were made ferocious representations of bestiality and black primitiveness. This imploding space, like the previous one discussed, reflected the aggressive conservative will to illuminate a new inner city youth.

Roving gangs, turf wars, drug deals, and violence dotted these streets. The conservative *Los Angeles Sentinel* (1985, 1986, 1989a, 1989b), for example, widely chronicled a new youth territorializing "blocks for drug sales," "alleys," "abandoned buildings," "vacant properties," "school yards," "parks," and "housing projects." Problem kids and violence-prone gangs seemed to affect every inch of inner cities. They struck suddenly, impulsively, and at unpredictable moments. While syndicated columnist Nicholas von Hoffman (1981) called black inner cities "a wasteland wherein children are trained to be muggers and hookers as thoroughly and effectively as white collar children are trained to be accountants," Isabel Wilkerson of the *Chicago Defender* has these places "crime [infested that has] become a savage intruder . . . on the toughest streets." In their wake, kids, families, and the elderly shuttered and struggled to stay safe (Wilkerson, 1989, A-12).

But this space, like others in the discourse, was a sophisticated human construction. It was the outcome of a sequence and a set of maneuvers (imposing silences, spotlighting presences, staging a coherence and clarity) that played to stereotypes. It banished to oblivion any subject or thing that contradicted this thematic space—non-gang youth, nonviolent gangs, normative kids, calm residents, families not huddling in houses. Also banished from this space was any sense of disadvantaged kids: youth reeling from poverty, inequality, racism, and hopelessness. As projected reality, this space bolstered conservative assertion. Its content more reflected human choreographing than the act of human reporting. This construction, ultimately inseparable from its makers' values and beliefs, was a potent politics.

Conservatives, especially national columnists and commentators, also often underscored gang ghastliness by muting these "turfs." Instead of providing precise locations for gang activity and drug sales, discussions often identified general markers: "abandoned houses in neighborhoods," "inner city alleys," "community streets," and "street corners." The gang threat, this way, was established but precise coordinates were made unknown. What was unencodable was communicatively crucial. This space, both clear and ambiguous, ultimately communicated a scary youth in glaring demonstration of realities (existence of gangs, their mobile character) and unknown possibilities (where these gangs were, where they could strike). This mix of clarity and ambiguity was the right formula to perpetuate a stereotype of culturally-spatially infected kids: They could be right around the corner. As conservatives demonstrated, making traditional Euclidean space could be powerful politics.

Conservatives in these ways imposed a massive silence on a diverse youth. Situating them in a place of habitation (the inner city), at a vulnerable age (youth), and in dubious class and cultural immersion made "them" counter-societal and ominous. Kids in Watts (Los Angeles), Hough (Cleveland), South Central Los Angeles, Harlem (New York), Central Ward (Newark), and Jeff-Vander-Lu (St. Louis) appeared as identical. Wherever conservatives looked, these kids were the same. Diversity had no place in the discourse; introducing richness and heterogeneity contradicted the offered coarse monolith. This reductionism, vitally strategic, reinforced the sense of easily categorizable black youth.

But because this scripting could be interpreted as raw conservative hatred rather than the core unblinking truth, by Sidney H. Schanberg's (1985) "unconscionably virulent conservatives," these kids were provided a thin veneer of civility for people to see through. National columnists and commentators and local politicians were most conscious of this veneer. They frequently made these kids superficially civilized, providing them with a vague comprehension of existing, in the words of conservative voice Rush Limbaugh (1992), "in worlds and lives of difference." But as true disabled creatures, to Limbaugh, they were said "to know little about what this difference was and lacked any sincere thought of changing." These kids were thus projected to circulate across inner cities bearing a vague semblance of civility, but, in what really mattered, had their minds, souls, and aspirations buried in depravity. These conservatives thus chronicled a generic inner city kid who, to *San Francisco Chronicle* writers

S. Fernandez and S. Matier (1988), barely felt, reflected, and thought as he or she pursued the likes of "a narrow quest for clothes, cars, and whatever pleasures the streets offer at the moment."

Inner city black youth were to be both taken for granted and an object of unending concern. People were to take for granted what they were; this identity was beyond doubt and further interpretation. Conservative depictions faithfully captured their essence. But people had to be concerned about these "mobile, intimidat[ing] kids" who were counter-societal and could not be ignored. These brutish bodies and brutish minds were predisposed to being violent, as escalating rates of black-on-black violence clearly showed. Like bait, they were cast out as a trap (as deformed, angry, and prone to impulsive violence) to lure the public into a feeding frenzy of anger and repugnance. As conservatives had represented urban issues before (see Males 1997), the core of the violence issue was a supposedly unstable youth freely and unapologetically choosing violence.

Inner City Black Family

The conservative discourse of "black-on-black violence" also narrated another key destructive source for violence-prone black youth: inner city black families. This family was made fundamental to this violence as an active transmittive agent of destructive ghetto values to kids. Ghetto space seared them with hideous results: destructive morals, temperament, and demeanor easily passed from parent to child. This key construct deepened the base for understanding a violence-prone black youth, connecting a youth to perceptions of his or her timeless shaper, the family. The result was to lodge this construction of kids in Norman Fairclough's (1992) mode of rationality. This rendition of family, following Fairclough, helped frame and ground the principal villain: black kids. It, like other support objects, was mobilized to make "real" a rendition of inner city black kids.

This black family was provided perverse characters: "welfare mothers," "absent fathers," "hardened teens," and "on-the-dole parents." Like past presentations of this family, this one attacked their morals and normality. But this post-1980 construction was distinctive in the ascribed intensity of dysfunctionalism. To Robin D. G. Kelley (1997), conservatives once had these parents basically aware of societal norms but struggling unsuccessfully to keep families intact. Post-1980, their awareness had disintegrated. To columnist Thomas Sowell (2001), an avid conservative commentator on black-on-black violence, underclass families "are marked by . . . emptiness, agonies, violence and moral squalor." This was Sowell's problem family, "decimated by three decades of disabling programs, welfare bailouts and affirmative action." Now, to Sowell, these families were often lost in the haze of a destroyed ghetto.

Mothers were spotlighted as the leading edge of this imploding family. They were embittered and discordant but retained a shred of maternal decency and hope. Commentator Rush Limbaugh frequently chastised these mothers: While "looking to find a better way," they "unsuccessfully played multiple parenting roles," "[gave] inconsistent discipline," "teach delinquency," and "were apologists for how their kids turned out." Often the staging offered a caricatured intimacy, like subject Dona Williams, who was interviewed in Harlem by *New York Times* writer Felicia A. Lee on "a streetcorner" and found "trying to keep things together" (Lee 1996, 17). Such women, to Lee, "never attended high school . . . [have] no marketable skills . . . [stay] home knitting and watching bootleg horror films as family members stop by . . . have eyes [that] are ancient." The dilemma was that kids turned elsewhere to meet their moral, social, and spiritual needs: peer groups, gangs, buddies.

Constructions of black family members were nuanced. They tended to intermix an old cultural form—the aimless, poor black wanderer—with a more recent form—the low-income black urban contagion—to produce hybrid characters (see hooks [1993] on these cultural forms). As wanderers, the central characters (post-1980 fathers and mothers) were shiftless beings: fathers were unremorseful migrants from responsibility, mothers were dreamers of a potentiality to wander. To Rush Limbaugh (1995), "Fathers often do not like family life and didn't hesitate to leave and not look back. [They] looked for an out in a world that they too often did not understand." "Mothers," to Limbaugh, "often reluctantly raised kids . . . their misery in staying put was often undeniable." The insinuation was cutting: Fathers looked for the next high or thrill outside the family; mothers lost themselves in lives of escapism (drugs, welfare dependency, TV, and sci-fi addiction).

One imagined space anchored this constructing: the "false-consciousness ghetto." Again, a remake of the urban inner city produced another space that satisfied a crucial narrative requirement. This space's momentary appearance, offered during discussion of black families, gave way to other spaces with other discourse things narrated. These families, chronicles communicated, carried and transmitted this false-consciousness ghetto in their ways and social fabric. It was seared into their visions, views, and temperaments. Everyday acts—failure to instill morals in kids, communicating relativist ethics, mothers and fathers living for the moment—built but also reflected this space. In their wake they produced an abhorrent space and, most importantly, aberrant kids.

The offering was nothing new: Decades of ethnographic exposés, stark policy pronouncements, and commentaries had mentally stunted wandering families infected by spatial fabric. In the 1960s, portrayals of inner city black families typically placed them in "culturally disoriented ghetto space" (see Abrahams 1964). This space confused and stymied black families as a created product of their actions. In the 1970s, this family was often narrated via horrific tales of a space's latest dilemma: public housing. This new positioning tied these families to a "project-afflicted ghetto space" as "project families," "inner city welfare households," and "ghetto families" that reinforced the sense of them as core problem in inner cities (see Jarrett 1974; Merridew 1975a).

Conservatives built on this narration in their post-1980 "black-on-black violence" discourse with the false-consciousness ghetto space. Ghetto cultural life had supposedly severely deteriorated and human cognition was devastated. Icons of bizarre culture and horrendous family decision-making littered it: unsupervised streets, dandyist men on street corners, free-to-roam youth gangs, drug-dealing parks, gang-colonized schools, and abandoned buildings. This space communicated out-of-control underclass culture and destructive family choices that damaged kids. With black families invoked, this distinctive space was illuminated in elaborate detail. As guest writer Eric Raymond (1990, 19) wrote in the

Philadelphia Inquirer, "[in black inner cities] young black males [suffer from] a maelstrom of drugs, violence, and broken families. Who will wake up the poor blacks [and families] in our cities to the fact that they've become their own worst enemies, [with kids] slaughtering each other in numbers the Klan could only dream of, yearly racking up casualty figures reminiscent of a medium-sized war?"

Imagined mental spaces helped make this rendition of black family one more way: they anchored a produced history to know them. A key space, the past ideal ghetto, was part and parcel of a narrated past that was important to constituting this family. A frequently discussed history of inner city black families had at its center a once serene ghetto space that encompassed once serene black families. This assembled text was the mythic remembrance of a family and community to know the current plight of these families. As a potent disciplining space, this black inner city history castigated its intended victim: current black families. Once good inner cities bred stable families; recently emergent bad inner cities bred troubled and dysfunctional families. These past spaces were the nostalgic terrains of the good old days, present spaces the unraveled environments of family and youth. As went space, so did its families.

National commentators notably waxed philosophic on these imagined serene ghettos. Once, according to commentator Rush Limbaugh (1992), "the black community had pleasant parks, safe streets, and well-maintained homes. . . . Poverty and economic hardship characterized black families and the ghetto . . . but were handled in moral and dignified ways." People were poor, but "these communities had morals and civility." People here "always struggled," but "obstacles were negotiated through community support, spirit, and constructive values." This was the black inner city's projected glistening past. As before, a luminous and seemingly benevolent space activated the desire to discipline. It unleashed a drive to punish as it communicated the magnitude of current family fall. In this sense, this space was not a passive window, but a staged pathway to affect public awareness.

Part and parcel of these once healthy spaces were what *Los Angeles Sentinel* columnist Elizabeth Wright (1988) called "clear parenting roles that "[offered] stable home lives and moral codes." Black families were effective regulators that "practiced nourishment of the mind and body." Fathers and mothers oversaw as concerned citizens. Fathers committed to family often disciplined and punished. Mothers concentrated on the intricacies of child rearing: nurturing egos, building moral character, monitoring friends and influences, and keeping drugs out of the house. These parents, socially assimilated, knew society's expectations and performed dutifully. The world was simpler then; black inner cities and society were culturally aligned. Standards of social conduct were universal, responsibilities broadly shouldered by all, and excessive diversity and relativism did not exist.

Again, conservatives imposed their own mix of presences and absences to yield a coherent product. Admittance into this space required people and objects to carry communicative thematic content. Indicators of conservative normalcy—drug-free streets, safe blocks, moral families, community-minded citizens, upstanding kids—inundated this space (they were of course barred from this space and replaced by indicators of pathologies in the post-1980 constructing of this space). This space, thus layered with self-supporting icons, collectively projected conservative truths about this family. Conservatives, borrowing from Henri Lefebvre (1984), were "doctors of space." Like architects and planners who explicitly work and rework actual physical space, these narrativists coded and recoded an imagined space to their specifications.

This space, of course, represented an actual historical landscape whose content grew more ambiguous and debatable over time. It was a decades-old terrain that existed before 1965. Yet conservatives were not fazed by the fade of time and declared a thorough knowledge of it. To use the past as a weapon against the present ("current destroyed black inner cities and families"), this past space had to be made easily read and known. In this context, conservatives ran roughshod over any sense of a contradictory reality: a difficult-to-decipher ghetto, a place with complex and contradictory meanings, a space whose content defied easy communication. Any possibility these issues even existed was obliterated. The history of ghettos was aggressively forwarded as always decipherable and easily explained. The goal was to offer an incisive historical text that could be used to reflect exactly what conservatives wanted.

With this making of black families, anger and rage flowed out of numerous conservative expositions. Some implored black families to do better; others went further and suggested that society find a way to penalize pitiful parenting skills. To the often conservative *Los Angeles Sentinel* (1989a), "Perhaps we have been trying to jail the wrong people. We have been spinning our wheels, trying to find a way to send the juveniles to jail. But we should have been looking at the parents." The *Sentinel* goes on: "We have listened to the parents as they have given all manner of excuses, but if the parents were made to pay, then they would see their children in a different way." In this plea, parents could do much better as role models and helpers of youth. They, as much as anyone and anything, were responsible for escalating black–on–black violence and other ghetto ills.

The Virulent Processes

The conservative discourse also offered virulent processes that paired up with its cast of villains to illuminate its "black-on-black violence" rendition. Again, constructions worked through and extended prevailing understandings and truths to give the public facts and realisms about this violence. A conceptual road map was unveiled whose navigation by the public led them to the inevitable destination: the irrefutable logic of conservative declaration. Multiple virulent processes—the operation of black underclass culture, inner city everyday life, the myth of racism—were assembled like pieces in a puzzle to naturalize a vision. Class, race, and space were again mobilized for a purpose: to bring people back to the "truths" of their instincts about poor black youth already caricatured and simplified in common thought.

Declining Inner Cities

A core virulent process woven into the discourse helped frame this "black–on–black violence" offering: declining inner cities. This general construct, a key set-up piece, moved through presentations as the expansive, downtown zone of eroding districts and neighborhoods that slid into its logical conclusion: "disorganized communities with problem kids."

This general low zone in the mapped-out urban topography provided a logic for the existence of disorganized kids. It "revealed" a seamless shading of aging, declining zones into "the block[s] . . . of the black underclass . . . with its own values, rules, and economy" (*New York Times* writer Felicia R. Lee 1989). This staging construct, repetitiously narrated, was symbolically crucial. Before there could be disorganized kids and neighborhoods, I suggest, there had to be decrepit inner cities.

Portraits of inner cities cast a spotlight upon aged and obsolescent places that carried the ominous imprint of economic decay and low-income African American habitation. These inner cities were minority-concentrated, heavy-industry areas that reproduced and refined long-term journalistic and media portrayals (see Still 1974). As urbanists have chronicled, early twentieth-century depictions of U.S. inner cities frequently reproduced a Dickensian cityscape of crowded, teeming, and disorganized zones and neighborhoods (see Boyer 1983). Middle-century narrators and beyond often served up tired and aging industrial spaces (see Beauregard 1993). The former invoked images of the Great Unwashed and dirty spaces, the latter zones of economic obsolescence. Both constructs had these areas formed through rounds of absorbing immigrants, industries, and poor households. They helped establish common understandings of inner cities on which this conservative discourse built.

Post-1980 conservative portrayals of inner cities took numerous forms. Some were steeped in vivid contrasts with "healthier" metropolitan spaces, for example suburbs, stable neighborhoods, blue-collar enclaves. A comparative frame, overtly identified, provided inner cities content and meaning. Other portrayals isolated inner cities as distinctive worlds and spotlighted absolute, raw decline. Elaborate renditions of gaping deterioration, in neighborhoods, streets, and industrial districts, were the norm. Still other portrayals spurned presentations of fixed, decrepit spaces to display dynamic, in-flux fall. These spiraling-downward spaces were sensationalized by being provided a raw rapid transformation. One example of each portrayal illustrates:

> In Detroit . . . you can see the decay in the commercial areas. It is debilitating to be constantly surrounded by this urban blight and this decay.

[In this context], the underclass . . . lives. (*Michigan Chronicle* writer Imani Humphrey 1992, A-5)

Unlike . . . our growing suburbs . . . one of the challenges in inner cit[ies] which is more or less universal is the problem of poverty and . . . a false sense of values. Everywhere one looks in America there are broken or wounded families, but the black inner city has more than its share. Here . . . Black men . . . are rarely at home. One man might have children by as many as half a dozen women. Although he occasionally visits these children, chances are that he is not a full time companion to any of their mothers. (freelance writer John A. Vieth 1990)

Flight from the city has become dramatic: pockets of poverty have been created where these were once flourishing residential communities . . . Drugs and crime are more noticeable . . . In addition, schools are being turned into social service agencies, with education as an almost secondary function . . . the culture of success that built this great country will survive outside the city. The [inner] city will decline, led by the culture of failure that blacks seem to have adopted as their destiny. (*Suppressed News* writer Jim Jackson 2001, 4)

But all of these narrativists were allied in making inner cities living, animate zones plagued by consumptive degeneracy. Inner cities unapologetically "ate" societal resources as engulfers of goods, services, and subsidies. One was to know this area by imagining above all else out-of-control consumptive beings. Indianapolis politician Carl Moldthan (1987), for example, said: "Indianapolis's inner city . . . consumes society's good will and resources at a dizzying rate. . . . It . . . asks for more and more resources as it struggles to survive. . . . subsidies are continually used but seem to have little effect." Like hedonistic and out-of-control organisms, this inner city mindlessly consumed with little remorse. In this zone's neighborhoods, "people race after pleasure of any kind, whatever is out there." To Moldthan, "kids, teenagers, and adults aggressively strike out to have fun and excitement . . . do drugs . . . join gangs." Mindless consumption, now, was the new reality that made this space different from others.

A key mental space, "consumptive inner cities," represented this urban environment. It was populated with people and land uses that advanced conservative designs. On the population front, all kinds of consumptively out-of-control people populated this space ("tawdry hookers," "absentee fathers," "welfare mothers," "homeless men," drugged-up kids"). These people were decimated and continued to consume ravenously. On the land-use front, abandoned houses, run-down parks, deteriorating buildings, and derelict industrial properties dominated. All of these needed maintenance, public dollars, and societal monitoring (see Denby 1986; Beverly 1991). The residential and nonresidential parts of this inner city space "ate" a litany of things endlessly and mindlessly: "government subsidies," "civic energies," "crack and other drugs," "decrepit media images," "the public dole," and "booming sadistic music." These things, the lifeblood of these spaces, drank this stuff up like they mindlessly consumed everything else, in large nonreflexive gulps.

This consumption was ultimately condemnation. Inner cities, communicated as deficient beings, were seduced by the superficiality of immediate gratification and lost in a cultural wilderness. A place had become like its inhabitants: culturally downtrodden and socially dysfunctional. Here, in brick and mortar, a metaphorical "false consciousness" blanketed a space. Like dazed and confused organisms, they pressed forward intent to consume. They knew little else and, befitting low-class, racial organisms, lived for the moment. This representation, a powerful politics, converted an inanimate materiality into a living, brooding, irresponsible being.

But offering consumptive inner cities also relied upon another mental space: "normative suburban terrain." Offerings of inner city, flagrantly comparative or not, used this space. This construct, a relational tool, was a disciplining device on the current inner city as a comparative benchmark. Exemplifying civility and normalcy in common thought, it was ideal for being mobilized to constitute inner city content (see Shields 1991, 1997; Creswell 1996). Its character, a robust economic base with a serene middle-class aesthetic and progressive culture, represented in common imagining an ideal community. Following Peter Stallybrass and Allan White (1986), offering this "high" allowed display of "the low." From its civilized people to its glistening buildings, current inner cities in comparison appeared raw, aged, and decrepit.

This suburban space seamlessly moved in and out of the discourse in references to ideal neighborhood. Discussions of inner cities typically invoked this ideal, replete with short description. For example, as Chicago city planners Don Lucas and Lee Thomas noted:

> What are we to make of inner cities today? I think they're a problem . . . places that have fallen far from the norm. Those that can move and jobs that can move do so and go to more livable environments where there's safety and security. . . . Here there's no fear of guns, drugs, the kind of things that's running through inner cities today. (Lucas 1991)

> Inner cities across America, I think, have not lived up to their promise. Where there could be nice homes, cohesive culture, and safe places, you know, the streets, schools that we take for granted in suburbs, they're often dingy and lacking the most common of things that many [people] are used to. (Thomas 1991)

This suburban space, Mike Davis (1990) chronicles, has been a long-term creation profoundly resonant in common thought. This template of bourgeois values and aspirations (see Davis 1990) has been propelled forward by TV, movies, books, and civic boosterism. It has come to symbolize the dominant postwar indicator of the impenetrable class divide, a place not substantially permeated by minorities and poverty. Its association with economic vibrancy, normative families, traditional values, and stable communities has made it, to Elizabeth Alexander (1996), the ideal instrument with which to batter other communities. This space, not surprisingly, is commonly mobilized to structure what all neighborhoods and communities are supposed to be. DuBose Brunner (1999) identifies this space as the key cog in a historic machinery of representation that has been continuously used to define non-normative communities.

But construction of declining inner cities was bolstered by one more space in the discourse: the landscape of past inner city rupture. A purported inner city economic and social implosion between 1970 and 1980, writer Charles Murray's (1984) dramatic inner city collapse, was widely narrated as a dramatic historical "event" that shaped current inner cities. This space was the 1970s dilemma of multiplying abandoned factories, falling-apart houses, unemployed men, and troubled kids in inner cities. Such use of "rupture space," following Anne Norton (1993), is a kind of ploy, extrematization, that can effectively ground presentations of current places. Such rupture offers dramatic falls or declines that situate a place's present in a key "fact" about its past. A cataclysmic event in a space's history, ultimately, helps understand its present condition.

This space was richly chronicled. In this era, to Chicago politician Devira Beverly (1991), "downtowns began to fall apart and communities were rocked to the core by a severe deterioration. . . . Housing and social networks were the principle victims in this that damaged inner cities from which they have yet to recover." The tear, to conservative narrativists, was not an isolated upheaval but the worsening of a long-term trend that spoke to the realities of present (1980s) inner cities. "If you want to know why downtown St. Louis is the way it is today," conservative St. Louis planner Joe Plann (2000) noted, "just look at what the 1970s did to them. . . . They are a mess because the 1970s wreaked havoc on them . . . Inner city decline started way before that . . . but housing and social conditions really plummeted at this point." To Plann, "kids became more unstable and started this 'black-on-black violence' stuff, that is what the 1970s gave to St. Louis."

An important support in these portrayals of ruptured spaces was language. Discussions used a wealth of image-rich terms to anchor their constructions. For example, conservative St. Louis politician Rik Mallory (1991) drew on diverse, luminous words to authenticate inner city rupture: "decrepit city blocks," "urban renewal eyesores," "sprawling housing complex[es]," and "hulking strangers on . . . crowded public streets." This language trapped memories and images in what Mikhail Bakhtin (1981) calls "the archive" of terms that were easily decoded. In Rush Limbaugh's (1995) 1970s reminiscences, moreover, "black neighborhoods were going to hell in a handbasket with its violent crime, blocks of housing abandonment, and rotting public housing." Public housing neighborhoods were falling apart," according to Limbaugh, with "abandoned buildings and drug houses all over." What had supposedly emerged in 1970s inner cities was supported by use of image-rich terms. With these offered icons of deterioration, 1970s inner city social and physical tear seemed beyond doubt.

The message in context was clear: 1970s imploding inner cities were an undeniable reality that led to a deterioration of downtowns and their black neighborhoods. With inner cities plummeting, their residential spaces also fell. Now horrendous black-on-black violence and other ills in these communities had easily identified roots that were local and easily read. This was important: a local deterioration ("disorganized black neighborhoods") linked to another local deterioration ("declining inner cities") obliterated any sense of impacts and influence from broader structural forces. Comments by St. Louis planner Joe Plann (2000) sum up this expedient obliterating: "black ghettos in the 1980s became poorer, more volatile, more cancerous . . . these underclass communities eroded when America's inner cities fell and kind of took these communities with them . . . in my mind, the roots of underclass formation are not difficult to see."

Racism

The final virulent process narrated to infuse the discourse with conservative meaning was the notion of racism. This construct, another key set-up piece, communicated a sense of a dramatic contraction of bigotry in urban America and the reality of minimally constricted youth. This notion moved through presentations as a greatly reduced racial animosity toward blacks in cities and society that tinged every depiction of person and process. The theme was resonant: Racism now persisted in public thought via rhetoric and social construction that politics and politicians kept alive. The theme "spoke" about diverse people and things in its suggestions of black false consciousness: liberal politicians, black values, black ways, black families, black consciousness, and liberal social policy. Its content ultimately reverberated across the totality of the discourse to provide key foundational meaning.

These discussions of racism were tightly bound to criticizing two things: liberal black politicians and general black thought. These staked-out things supposedly kept this concept alive and ultimately sanctioned the individual acts that led to "black-on-black violence." One, a person, and the other, a state of consciousness, were said to dwell excessively on the popular and superficial. To the conservative Chicago University Village Association (UVA) (1991), a once virulent racism had declined "and the real problem now was politicians, advocates, and easily persuaded people." Racism, under the guise of recognizing need for equal treatment, violated this very tenet. By invoking this need, careers were made, bureaucracies expanded, and resources acquired by political operatives for personal gain. For an American mainstream acutely sensitive to the rhetoric of minority-racial privilege post-1980, this was potent stuff.

But this attempt to subvert the legitimacy of the concept "racism" was nothing new. Since the 1960s, with the dramatic emergence in popular thought of the notion of racism, conservatives aggressively strived to negate this notion that was central to liberal legislative successes: for example, the civil rights movement, the Great Society, and the national busing movement (see Steinfels 1979; Pinckney 1990). In the discourse, this demise of racism, like previous accounts, celebrated triumphant societal virtuousness over vice, which greatly reduced racist thought and action. Indeed, to the most strident conservatives on this "black-on-black violence" issue, even engaging race in discussions of urban issues was seamy. It was an abhorrent site of ideology and advocacy politics. To syndicated columnist Thomas Sowell (1984), a figurehead in this engagement, those who dwelled on race in dialogue about black-on-black violence were "political hucksters, liberal thinkers, misguided and misled poor people." To columnist Walter Williams, dwelling on race, "in the name of half-baked sociological theories, and perverted ideas of justice, accomplishes nothing but [gives] criminals carte blanche to prey on society" (Williams 1985, 12).

Here was the use of Peter Ehrenhous's (1993) tyrannizing power of the therapeutic motif. This ploy uses the idea of therapy and healing to discipline people to accept a supposed undeniable truth. Once, to conservatives, American society had failed to act in ways consistent with its democratic ideals. But in recent times society had substantially purged its bestial instincts. Now, African Americans were to feel better about society and their place in it as people provided with new possibility. Society had changed; now inner city blacks were to respond. Poverty, violence, and black anger were now deemed inexcusable; to suggest disabling institutions or social structures was rhetoric. The idea of racial constraints on life chances were to be barred from acceptable public dialogue; myth had no place in public discourse. Black youth, contextualized this way, were made creators of their conditions in a new liberating, modernist reality.

But this racism construct, like others in the discourse, relied on Lefebvre's spaces. One, the past racist landscape, "slavery space," was especially critical. This space, identified as the reality of once active racism, appeared widely in the discourse and communicated a profound progress in race relations. National columnists and commentators notably made and used this historic landscape to communicate what racism was and its timely demise. This landscape, in discussions of racism, was fronted and narrated as racism's embodiment. Where there was racism, this landscape existed. When there was racism, this landscape was prominent. But in a strategic communicating, this space had vanished across America. Once prevalent but subsequently gone, it functioned as a metaphor for racism: eliminated from the present, eliminated from reality.

This construct offered racism as a once overt racial enslavement in a popularized image: the Old South plantation. It conveyed a zone of human plunder that showed the physical expression of racism for all to see. Racism was in the orderliness of country estates, the shanties of slaves, the trading posts for the exchange of human property, and the haughty display of wealth in homes and properties. It took people to a bygone time and place, what radio voice Rush Limbaugh (1995) called "the Old South," "the era when cotton was king," "a time when plantations dominated the south," "when whips and oppression were commonplace practices of landowners." Limbaugh, using this imagined space, discussed racism as "a kind of life when people were property and used for their labor to raise crops and do other kinds of menial work." The tactic was effective: tied to one visualization, racism was centered within one social life (agrarian living) and one social relation (master–slave relation).

In this way, racism was condensed to a region, one kind of plundering, one kind of relation, and one kind of spatial imagining. This process, to Rush Limbaugh (1995), "ravaged the soul of black people on sprawling plantations in an unsettling ownership of human property that thankfully no longer exists." To Limbaugh, racism was when "blacks had the status of cattle on plantations, when they could be purchased and sold like commodities." But with blacks no longer on plantations and these largely a past thing, by insinuation, racism disappeared. This imagined space, so served up, was a text that displayed what once was and how social realities had changed. It marked social relations through assembling coded indicators— country estates, plantation houses, cotton fields, slave quarters—that advanced conservative politics.

This "slavery space" was used because it was a creation embedded in common thought and could be strategically used. It was the common image of southern plantation living in the antebellum period that was America's central icon for slavery. Its creation, in movies, TV, newspapers, and novels across the decades that can be dubbed the *Gone With the Wind* phenomenon, came to assume its place as a dominant representation of slavery and racism. Conservatives knew this space and excavated it from common comprehension. The space put into play thereby became an "instrumental space," mobilized to advance conservative thought. It was not intrinsically conservative, but in this use became a conservative political tool. It, like other representations of space used, flickered in and out of discourse depending upon what was momentarily being discussed. With racism discussed, it appeared; when another aspect of this violence was being discussed, it disappeared.

But conservatives made and worked through another key mental space, black suburbanization, to bolster their presentation of racism. Black exodus from American cities had intensified in the 1970s (Muller 1981; Palen 1995). Conservatives widely discussed this exodus in their "black-on-black violence" discourse. This discussing offered a new metropolitan landscape resonant with stark truths about opportunities and possibilities for inner city blacks. Writers like Joseph Perkins and Thomas Sowell widely discussed black suburbia. Newspaper editorials and think-tank reports did the same (see Heritage Foundation 1998; *American Prospect*

1998). This space was used as a key truth teller that cut through rhetoric and mystification to demonstrate new possibilities for blacks. Indianapolis planner Angelo Franceschina (1987) put it best: "If we were to know about race and racism," he said, "the tale of black suburbanization had to be told."

This illuminated black suburb was the new terrain of opportunity for enterprising blacks. It was wonderfully clean, aesthetically pleasant, middle-class black, and politically moderate. It differed from other suburbs only in racial content. Black suburban space, to Indianapolis mayoral candidate Carl Moldthan (1987), was "neat rows of homes that dotted tree-lined streets just like other suburban communities." This "new middle-class black reality provided African Americans with their piece of the suburban pie. . . . Its houses and neighborhoods were the stuff black families and others dreamed of." "There was a new mobility in the [urban] black community," Moldthan said. "[R]acism had subsided and black suburban tracts had exploded all over the place." Here were the black families, according to Rush Limbaugh (1995), that "refused to buy into racism," "rejected strangulating ideology and destructive welfare rhetoric," and "left the bad for the good."

In conservative discussion, this space was a middle-class, monolithic entity. There was no poverty or low-wage economy here (no Wal-Marts, Sams, gas stations, Hardees, sweatshops), only the icons of middle-class living. Banished to oblivion were ghettos, low-wage stores and factories, low rent zones, and socioeconomic diversity, the outcome of political maneuvers (imposing presences, invoking silences, creating a monolithic unity) that staged a coherence and clarity. This narrating, forwarding an idealized community that the public could respect, offered less an actual, reported-on community than Mike Davis's (1990) creation of a residential fantasy. Its content supported assertion about new opportunities for blacks and the demise of racism; it potently advanced conservative politics.

This black suburbanization construct slammed African American racialist thought. It allowed many conservative voices to express shock that blacks or anyone else could believe in virulent racism. "It speaks for the state of existing thought," said the head of Chicago's University Village Association (1991), "that some still entertain the notion of a destructive racism." Conservatives referenced their time-tested folk devil: a massive black false consciousness. Black folk, academics, politicians, and spokespeople were people being misled, having troubled grasping core truths, or simply staging self-serving realities. Here was supposed proof of people thinking in deficient and political ways who were unfit to offer serious comment on "black-on-black violence." "When we look at suburbs today, Indianapolis conservative politician Stu Rhodes said (1986), "the truth about racism is obvious. . . . The pill too many [can] not swallow [is] the reality of personal responsibility."

In this discourse one type of person most forcefully peddled this notion of racism: liberal black politicians. They were anointed the leaders of the untamed and uncontrollable black inner city voice. On the scheming side, frequent targets were Jesse Jackson, Coleman Young, Marion Barry, and Maxine Waters; the hopelessly misguided side featured Jesse Jackson (again), Michael White, Tom Bradley, David Dinkins, and Andrew Young. All supposedly peddled notions of racism and inequality as reasons for this violence, and tended to use a relativist liberal morality to maneuver ghetto residents to their side. Sometimes fiery rhetoric was used; at other times a resonant firmness. Styles of these politicians could vary, conservatives communicated, but the substance of their ideas did not.

But this construction of post-1980 liberal black politicians differed from previous ones. Once, as Tommy Lott (1999) chronicles, these politicians were marked as deficient and ineffective. In the 1960s, to Lott, they were made to look as though they lacked the smarts and savvy to maneuver effectively on behalf of ghetto residents. This post-1980 construct, in contrast, offered a more politically astute and coercive politician with flamboyant ways, glib persona, and smooth oratory. This was the era, the Reagan years and beyond, when conservatives spoke of welfare queens, slippery politicians, and free-loading black bucks dominating ghettos (see Reed 1992). Now a more gamy politician was on the prowl, one who used an unstated code of reciprocity to deliver resources for political support. This way, conservatives placed these politicians at the intersection of natural self-interest, materialist desire, political ambition, and talented hustling.

This constructing took two forms. First, there was flagrant assertion. Syndicated columnist Clarence Page (1984), for example, had these politicians as "those [people] who hold press conferences, fume and move on [to] leav[e] the problem [black-on-black violence]." To Eric Raymond (1990) in the *Philadelphia Inquirer,* "who will speak the hard truth: that . . . continued attempts at the moral blackmail of innocent whites [by black politicians] with reminders of past racism . . . [perpetuate] resentment, dependence on government largesse, and the victim syndrome." These narrativists fit the stereotype of blunt, no-holds-barred conservatives happy to blister liberals and minorities. They typically projected themselves as common populist people, and were "located" to easily read these politicians.

But many conservatives rejected such blatant discussion and communicated this politician's character as much around nuance and deft use of space. They again often turned to a time-tested object, the human body, to communicate this politician. Narrating the body, identities were collapsed into revealing gestures that resurrected again a familiar understanding: primitive black people. Reporting of body movements, waves of the hand, and especially vocal stylings suggested gamy politicians with concealed goals and motives. These movements, one more time, took readers to imagined inner city space that evoked notions of upbringing, styles of parenting, and character of community. In general terms, black politician bodies were offered as strong, inviolable, flexible, and transparent. Against an elusive ethos, conservatives communicated, this being could be read and understood.

One body part, the mouth, was displayed as this politician's most effective instrument for deception. No one's mouth was more singled out and vilified than the number one black liberal bad guy: Jesse Jackson. *National Review* writer Mark Steny (1999), for example, portrayed a shifty and opportunistic Jesse Jackson who "in sing-along[s] . . . puts PR in prayer . . . as he practices misplaced narcissistic opportunism." Steny discusses a style of speech that appeared to rage like wildfire to animate and arouse people. Similarly, *Commentary* writer Midge Dector (1992) had another liberal bad guy, Los Angeles congresswoman Maxine Waters, as an uncontrollable talker and theatricist. To Dector, "Maxine Waters, who had flown in from Washington [during the 1992 L.A. riots], could be observed rushing around in high spirits, cameramen in tow, crying out to her constituents how much she cared for them and exhorting them to trust her in return. . . . As one watched her skipping through the still-smoldering rubble, it was hard to banish the thought that probably never again had she had, and probably never again would she have, quite so good a time."

Conservatives communicated here at multiple levels. At one level, this was an attack on liberal black politicians and their articulations of racism. These community leaders were described as destructively shaping inner city black thought and misleading people about the causes for "black-on-black violence." People were to see one more carrier of black inner city confusion and disorganization that misspoke about "black-on-black violence." Another product of this space wore its destructive fabric and ways and could not see this violence's real causes. These politicians were always confident and brash, but the reality was another primitive being who could not shake a space and speak the truth.

But more deeply, conservatives used this example of a defective black politician to attack the consciousness of black kids. If political representatives were cognitively afflicted by this space, what about these kids? If trusted public officials from "the ghetto," the most educated and articulate of this population, carried the powerful imprint of the ghetto, didn't these kids as well? The message was clear: this damaging space ensnared all in its wake and made human agency aberrant and dysfunctional. All who resided here were influenced by it; subsequent social pathologies had to be seen as agency-driven and anything but surprising. "Black-on-black violence," then, was offered as individualistic and cultural. This was ultimately made a primitive act that logically flowed from a primitive setting teeming with primitive people. All that lived here were damaged, and black-on-black violence was not surprisingly an everyday reality.

The Final Product

This chapter documents that beneath seemingly simple and straightforward conservative discussions of "black-on-black violence" was an elaborate contextual setting-up. Brute articulations about deficient kids in dysfunctional neighborhoods concealed a constructed field of under-standing that laid out a supportive reality for conservative discussion. This reality of objects (for example, "black inner cities," "racism," "black fami-lies," "underclass culture," "black youth") authenticated conservative as-sertion. As in all discourses on social issues, discussed themes relied upon a supporting construction of reality. A narrated social issue, this way, drew strength from locking people into an inability to think beyond it rather than possessing an absolute validity. Such commonsense positioning, not absolute fact, anchored expressions of truth and cause.

Space helped craft the field of understanding as a widely used geo-graphical fabric. Its use as mental spaces served up realms of perception, imagination, and fantasy. Space was constituted as value-transmittal zones, geometric landscapes of proximities and potential interactions, past and present places of normalcy, texts of lurking villains and forces, and territo-ries of movement and transgression. Other innovative ploys of course helped build these objects, but space made in creative ways equally served conservative politics (see Soja 1989, 1996). Use of space to advance poli-tics is not the exclusive domain of conservatives; it can be used by all kinds of politics and can be applied to an infinite variety of political projects. But here, conservatives used this resource effectively, without which their political project would have proven much more difficult to undertake.

All of the objects discussed meshed in the conservative discourse to help create an unmistakable message: this violence was a dilemma in the realm of values. Potent meanings and images effectively staked this vio-lence to popular images of pathological culture and kids: predatory black youth, culturally and morally deformed black life, socially disorganized inner cities. These values were placed everywhere in inner cities: in kids, politicians, inner city spaces, minds, and sensibilities. The pervasiveness of this discourse deformed everything in its wake: bodies, dress, gestures, physical spaces, cognitive processes, and common imaginings.

This violence in narratives was ultimately situated in the heart of a normalized, vile world. It was offered as the new accepted way to express anger, offer self-expression, impose one's will, gain status, acquire identity, and survive. Within a vicious cycle of cultural and moral denigration, a cycle of violence had arisen. Its roots could be detected in the walk, talk, and attitudes of kids. The outside world, to conservatives, made this violence abhorrent and shocking. In black inner cities, it had become common and normative. Conservatives this way revealed a ghastly violence that had become logical and expected.

This constructing devalued black lives in bold strokes. Loss of black life by black-on-black violence was made a grisly but logical outgrowth of sinister culture. Loss of life was coded as expected, inexorable, the outcome of people's not trying hard enough to extricate themselves from destructive circumstances. For those that tried to escape, black suburbanization was the result. For those that didn't try, there were consequences. Inner city black lives in this presenting seemed expendable, a people who agreed through choice to dwell in dangerous, self-made cultures and terrains. That they would die in record numbers had to be expected. This violence, in the final analysis, was made to appear as a brutal symptom of a process on the verge of becoming horrifying in its potential to ravage mainstream life. In society, from this gaze, the violence was in an important way momentarily controlled but with the potential to spread and to become the ghastly societal menace that conservatives told the public to fear.

4

The Liberal Discourse

The General Gaze

Liberals too spoke widely about "black-on-black violence" after 1980. Pronouncements, framed as anti-conservative, discussed a shocking and tragic, albeit a potentially reversible, "black-on-black violence." These newspaper columnists, TV commentators, magazine writers, and local and national politicians ruminated about the sanctity of black life, the reality of black community potential, and loss of human life. Their most visible spokespeople made themselves sensitive to the community pain from black-on-black violence: Rick Bragg, Dr. Louis Sullivan, Michael Norman, Mike Royko, Nancy Jefferson, Eileen Ogintz, Geoffrey Canada, Bob Greene, Alex Kotlowitz, Nicholas Lehmann. They assumed a number of roles in the discourse: inner city truth-teller, progressive urban activist, and grieving observer. They purportedly spurned harsh and judgmental accounts of these kids, their proclaimed struggle to humanize them lending the discourse its moral core.

These liberals especially proclaimed themselves as challenging conservative explanations of black-on-black violence. Conservatives purportedly demonized kids through crude racial and class stereotypes; they examined inner cities deeply and unearthed causal nuance (complex kids, troubled communities, inadequate government resources, racism, and deindustrialization). This violence, again reduced to "black-on-black violence," was hailed as a complex process: they and not conservatives had their finger on the pulse of this complexity. Conservatives spoke from vague and stereotyped knowledge of inner cities, they from informed understanding and clear readings of inner city terrains. They struggled to know this world, interrogated its deepest recesses; conservatives were content to dispassionately see and quickly judge.

But articulation of differences can be more superficial than substantive. Again a supposedly new inner city reality—afflicted black culture and culturally off-the-map black youth—was put at the heart of "black-on-black violence." This was the supposedly astonishing new circumstance in America's inner cities that needed highlighting and reflecting upon. Drugs and crime inundated these places, underclass culture engulfed kids, and gangs proliferated. This discussing and embellishing, in the context of referencing contextual forces (for example, poverty, deindustrialization, racism), ultimately communicated this culture's dominance and obscured the other causal forces cited. This culture, again, featured stereotyped men, women, and children (welfare mothers, drug-peddling kids, dandyish men, disorganized families, culturally off-the-map kids) in bedraggled places.

Two kinds of presentations dominated this discourse: no-holds-barred reportage of black-on-black violence and discussions of problems and prospects in cities and black communities. No-holds-barred reportage of violence, first, featured, like conservative presentation, blunt and richly realistic truth-telling. But it displayed a more nuanced reality: one of deepened poverty, unemployment, youth anger, and horrendous youth decision-making. Yet these discussions became exercises in making sense of inner city culture and its impacts on youth. Discussions dwelled on "worlds" of puzzling values and lifestyles that interwove grisly and horrific images with expressions of tragedy and sadness. Immense pain in shocked communities dominated by pathological gangs and kids suffused the discussions. These ghastly environments tragically decimated humanity and left communities reeling. For example, *Michigan Chronicle* columnist Harry D. Pierson reports:

> I have just returned from Chicago . . . Jonathan Macon was laid to eternal rest. As we view the plight of Black youth, I am aware of their struggle for a common existence. Children are deprived of their childhood and education . . . Children have become pawns for the drug runners

and pushers. Children are armed and dangerous. Young toddlers have learned how to duck, run to safety upon hearing gunshots.

Today . . . the Black community is . . . divided and . . . this division has caused a deadly breakdown in the Black family structure. As we observed funeral processions going and coming, I wondered how many young people were going to their final resting place. (Pierson 1993, A-7)

Discussions of urban problems and prospects also communicated this violence as rooted in culture and horrific youth decision-making. More so than in the reportage of violence stories, it outlined a sense of root problems and causes. Contextual-societal forces (deindustrialization, spatial mismatch, welfare state contraction) and cultural influences (underclass values and lifestyles) were both commonly invoked. But the new inner city culture again dominated discussion and was provided most compelling imagery. It intermixed horror and tragedy ("the new underclass neighborhood") to make these kids objects of pity and dangerous sources of contagion. Cause, again, was all but collapsed into articulations and musings about the power of inner city culture. For example, thoughts of this violence by Cranston Knight in his piece "Thoughts on Black-On-Black Crime" in the *Chicago Defender* are illustrative. He writes:

"Violence in and of itself is horrible but what's even more horrible is the nihilism, narcissistic, and sociopathic behavior of the gunmen, many of whom can take another human life without any sign of remorse. Something is extremely wrong with any society when its youth can kill and not feel shame, guilt, or the pain that accompanies the pulling of a trigger.

[Some look for solutions.] Yet in their search for a solution, these men of goodwill looked at the African American community as if it were part and parcel of the United States. But it is not.

[Here is the dilemma.] With increased factionalization, many factories closed, relocated, or were either blown up or burned down. Men and women were left unemployed. In the ensuing breakdown of social order, families disintegrated, children were left without fathers (killed) and women were left to run the households.

As the social, psychic atmosphere became one of pure survival, sociopathic behavior developed and human life lost its value. Young men in their late adolescence joined rival groups, shooting at each other for no other reason than a rival group had entered their territory.

Youth gangs replaced the family. Violence became an everyday occurrence. Nihilism replaced human life. The hope for longevity, which is part of the normal adolescent growth period, was sublimated by an attitude of "live for today, and today only." Killing someone became a right of passage for many young men. (Knight 1994, 12)

Violence as Ghastly Youth Erosion

A fundamental theme anchored the discourse: the evolution of tragic but ghastly inner city youth. This theme narrated and fixated on a central subject to communicate this evolution: drug-peddling gangs. Through this subject, liberals communicated a horrific violence that mirrored the new social problem of kids and communities afflicted by gangs. Liberals, like conservatives, provided melodrama with stereotyped characters, rapid action, and extreme states of being. Confrontations of virtue and vice littered inner cities: stability had disappeared under the frenetic and sensational. The theme was resonant in connecting to established understandings of these kids. But while featuring this youth via gangs in the theme, discussion will show that this construction relied on building a liberal specific "field of understanding." These elements—the inner city, black culture, society, and politicians—platformed and provided meaning to liberal assertion. Each element ultimately gained meaning from each other as supportive and bolstering constituents.

Drug-Peddling Gangs

The central subjects in this liberal discourse, drug-peddling gangs, were made a failing group in economically devastated and culturally declining inner cities. Post-1980 liberal offerings of troubled youth in cities, according to Michael Keith (1993), often begin with notions of gang ways and cultures. Problem kids, to Keith, are connected to understandings of a destructive youth formation that is seen to shape and mold them. Such offerings, marking diverse discourses on education, housing, crime, safety, and others, typically serve up gangs as a leading edge of inner city decline (see Angone 1981; Gow 1993). This villainous force, in the liberal discourse, now dueled with families for the hearts and minds of kids. Gangs were winning, families were losing.

Gangs were said to be an outgrowth of a range of forces: deindustrialization, postindustrial society, and destructive racialization. But the prominent storyline was gangs engaged in ongoing and destructive social practices. Across neighborhoods, mobile kids tussled with corrective institutions: churches, Boys Clubs, legal aid societies, liberal politicians. To Karen P. Nolan (1993), a frequent writer on black-on-black violence for the *Chicago Defender,* "decency and civility were being overrun by street culture and gangs." Nearly spent local institutions—tenant groups, block clubs, neighborhood watches, Boys Clubs—fought desperately to curb their actions and "the deadly spiral of social disorganization." To Nolan, gang activities had spread to streets, schools, playgrounds, parks, the world of common sense.

Melodrama with rapid action and extreme states of confrontation permeated these depictions. Riveting tangles of pathologies marked these kids. A lurid cast of characters was featured: "angry kids," "unemployed men," "ex-cons," "idle youth," and "prisoners turned gang leaders." From dark and troubled origins (bad families, bad neighborhoods), gang members hailed. Upon membership, attempts to obtain group status and support led to a rapid downward spiral of drug selling and irrational violence. In this context, it took meticulous and energized policing to keep these feared gangs at bay. *New York Times Magazine* contributor Michael Norman, for example, writes on a typical day of a New York City cop in the Bronx:

In this setting, it was an achievement just to keep order. . . . Again . . . policemen Kevin Jett encountered one more bad [gang member]. Jett had only wanted to tweak the mutt, not force a duel. But one word has led to another and a line has been drawn, and now, too, from out of nowhere, come Killer's supernumeraries, five in all, among them a giant in a track shirt.

"Killer's feared around here, so every once in a while I got to bring him down a peg." And today, spotting him around the bend on Valentine, the officer has decided to do just that. "Hey! Killer!" The dealer wheels, his face sour, his eyes full of rage. "What you call me Killer for!" he snaps. "You know my name." (Norman 1993, 64)

But these gangs were distinctively made by being narrated through the lenses of consumption and production. This representing was powerful. These metaphors, to Anne Norton (1993), are ominous signifiers in American thought. To Norton, diverse, potentially problematic things are imagined to expand through consumption: foreign countries, territories, political systems, diseases, and armies. Consumption commonly invokes a sense of aggressiveness and expansive desires. Not surprising, the sense of the United States being consumed by invading nations, internal cultures, waves of immigrants, and its own excesses populates American mythology (see hooks 1993). Production, similarly, is a powerful signifier to portray underachievement and ineptitude. Through this portrayal, America's most marginalized populations have been symbolically ravaged (see Wilson and Grammenos 2000). Use of these metaphors in the discourse assigned dangerous connotations to these gangs. Both helped display aggression and lethargy that aided liberals in making these gangs markers of youth and community decline.

On the production side, in the discourse, gang members were in tatters. These deficient producers, according to *New York Times* columnist R. Bernstein (1988), "lacked jobs," "lacked skills," "couldn't conceive of the possibility of doing a hard day's work," and "gave the ghetto two things, problems and drugs." The quick and dirty selling of drugs, lucrative and easy, was their main entrepreneurial undertaking. Productive energies, were, to Chicago politician Nancy Jefferson (1991), chased out in a spectacle of "shrinking human initiative." Here was *New York Times* columnist Rick Hampson's (1986) "post-industrial Dark Age . . . hitting the street." These kids, "wounded by post-industrialism," reflected a "stunning breakdown of community, family, and work—the heart and soul of civilized society" (*New York Times* writer Charles E. Silverman 1994).

On the consumption side, gangs had evolved into Indianapolis Director of Metropolitan Development B. Call's (1987) "pathologically marauding group of bad kids." These gangs, to Call, "lived off others" and "ate up the streets and always wanted more territory." They "had an irrational drive to seize more turf," "plotted to occupy schools yards," "[initiated] gang spring recruiting drives," and "claimed public housing as their drug turf." This consumption, to Call, persisted despite societal sanction and public concern. Call's gangs in Indianapolis had been stripped down to "a coarse impulse" that left them crudely consumptive. Call, like other liberals, talked about the difficulties of these kids' plight and circumstance but in the next breath happily revealed profligate gangs needlessly "eating up" neighborhoods. These gangs, represented as ceaselessly devouring children, groped to understand themselves and the world they found bewildering.

But the offering of imagined spaces was at the heart of this constituting of drug-peddling gangs. A key imagined space repetitiously narrated anchored this making: "the historic serene ghettoscape." This made space, frequently narrated in detail, was the comparative benchmark to show this gang's current plight. Its displaying helped render these kids currently decrepit by juxtaposing images of past neighborhood and its youth against the present. Offers of once serene community, to Rob Shields (1991, 1997), can profoundly ground depictions of present people. This widely used instrument displays the past to discipline the current. Such idealized spaces, to Shields, help communicate "truths" of undeniable changes that locate a people's present in a key "fact" about its past. This past batters the present as a haunting reminder of what once was. The past, in this view, becomes a powerful political frame.

This imagined ghettoscape was infused with haunting images. It was provided clean, well-kept groups of blocks lovingly monitored by parents and relatives. Here, to Chicago's Por Un Barrio Mejor director Carlos Heredia (1992), people from stoops and windows "incessantly bantered on warm summer evenings . . . children played . . . people informally mingled in streets . . . kids recreated with pleasure in schoolyards." Social networks extended across communities that facilitated social monitoring. Families were whole and pure; fathers worked and mothers tended to youth needs. Sense of community imprinted everyone; house, block, and neighborhood were cherished associations. In this era, to academic writer William Julius Wilson, "Blacks in Harlem and in the ghetto neighborhoods did not hesitate to sleep in parks, on fire escapes, and on rooftops during hot summer nights . . . and whites frequently visited inner city taverns and nightclubs" (W. J. Wilson 1987, 3).

Here was Bruce Lincoln's (1989) tyranny of space and history that staged objective facts about these kids. Use of this space allowed liberal chronicles of these kids' social and cultural problems to assume a normalcy. Space and history, to Lincoln, commonly come together in constructions of landscape (neighborhoods, ethnic enclaves, communities) to judge and discipline current people. Here, historic spaces demonize present people and spaces by revealing their fall from normal states. The politics of these historic spaces, to Lincoln, are never revealed as they are invoked and batter the current. Idealized fragments are woven into a coherent space and declared a "once harmonious reality." In this process, assertions of current disorder depend upon establishing a relation with a human-contrived past space.

But these gangs also acquired meaning via use of another key space, "drug-dealing inner city space." A history of liberal discourses prior to 1980 sets the stage to fashion this space. In the 1960s and 1970s, liberal books, ethnographies, and magazine reports widely presented a place-based black youth struggling in a similar kind of inner city: a "crisis of disillusionment space" (see Moynihan 1966; *U.S. News and World Report* 1972a). Inner city neighborhoods were purportedly exploding: kids had become, in the words of writer Daniel Moynihan (1965, 1966), "troubled ghetto youth," "cultural products of ghettos," and "hardened inner city youth." This space seared them; many spiraled downward in a dramatic cultural deterioration. In the era of growing prosperity prior to 1980, it was narrated, U.S. society was going in one direction, these kids in another.

This "drug-dealing" space spotlighted the character of these gangs in a key maneuver: by collapsing this space into one prominent activity, dealing drugs. In this frequently narrated space, gangs members, often pre-teenagers, relentlessly peddled drugs on street corners and intimidated passersby in their actions. Crack cocaine was their leading ware: it was un-abashedly hawked on streets far and wide. In the process, gangs postured as assertive and authoritarian adults. A superficial world of display and posture had supplanted an authentic raw, roughneck ghetto. Kids now obsessed with consumptive acts hip-hopped across streets, circulated as brooding groups, eyed girls as trophies to be "won," exuded a hard-edged authority, and too often donned guns to fill nights with senseless gun-fire. This monolithic space banished any semblance of youth normalcy in it: kids with gang affiliations had degenerated into perverse entrepre-neurs mindlessly servicing the needs of gangs. Gangs, this way, were staged to recruit youth to their fold, facilitate the black community drug trade, destroy neighborhood moral and social order, and help escalate local violence.

This imagined space was filled with disturbing images. It was infused with open drug dealing in broad daylight that scarred streets, markets, schools, and local activity patterns. Here, to *Chicago Tribune* writer Ellen Ziff, we see "hous[es] on block[s] front for drug ring[s] . . . school park-ing lot[s] are . . . hangout[s] for youth gangs . . . people . . . pulling their shutters closed . . . growing concerns about crime" (Ziff 1981, 2). Drug selling bothered people going to the store, harassed the elderly in parks, and made street corners dangerous sites for potential violence. Every-where people walked, the grim reality of drug peddling was present. In this neighborhood, *Chicago Defender* . . . writer LaTicia Greggs tells, "young m[e]n . . . spot young women..[and] invite [them] to partake in [a] wide selection of illicit drugs . . . 'Yo, yo, miss ladee, need a dime bag? Got that ready rock? What'tch want is what I got,' they tell others" (Greggs 1992, 1).

But this drug-peddling gang space was made a site of memory as well as ruin, with important repercussions. As a shaping influence on kids, it was something simultaneously memorialized and decimated. The making was deft: Amid anger, posture, absence, dereliction, and dysfunction, frag-ments of the past remained. Parks, streets, kids, families, and open spaces were battered and failing but still retained a shred of normalcy. Kids were just thoughtful enough, streets still carried a semblance of civility, gangs operated like primitive businesses, so that they hinted at what once was. This inclusion, a characteristic of liberal discourse on inner city issues, was an outgrowth of liberal impulse to make minority and ethnic spaces nostalgic (Kennedy 2000; David Wilson 2001). Its effect in the discourse was important: it accentuated the intensity of the youth and community fall. In the same location, one could see the high and the low, what once was as an ideal set against what was now.

In sum, these liberals curiously treated this youth: understanding them through the centering of gangs, compassion was allocated, but to restless perpetrators who seemed more wild and wooly than deprived. Notions of context and struggle punctuated presentations, but of a fantastically out-of-control social group (gangs) and youth. Again, inner city fears and fantasies were mapped onto this terrain. These kids, amid detail, remained an abstract phenomenon, what Liam Kennedy (2000) calls a socio-psychological fantasy. This mix of faithful reportage (liberal understandings) and intentional political caricature (to invoke alarm about a black youth crisis) made these kids ghastly, which had the effect of curtailing reason for societal involvement. Liberals this way duplicated conservative contentions of culture-infected kids. This gang-seared youth, ultimately carnivalized for their differences from the mainstream as a monolithic racial category, replenished stereotype.

Hope and Possibility for Eradicating Violence

But there was another central theme in the discourse: hope for reversing black-on-black violence. Set against staggering inner city youth and communities, objects supporting this theme revealed possibilities to stem black-on-black violence. With this second theme, the discourse interwove graphic reality, communicated through previously discussed objects, with optimistic possibility, offered through about-to-be-discussed objects. Liberals desired to do more than portray declining youth and communities; possibilities for lessening this violence had to be forwarded. Mobilizing full-scale societal intervention to tackle black-on-black violence, a deep liberal desire, required chronicling both the ill and the possibilities for its reversal. The discourse, paraphrasing Bakhtin (1981), needed the problem, the solution, and the salvationist to be whole and to embody liberal sentiment. "Space of hope" objects in the discourse that I now examine—racism, black leaders, black culture—completed the liberal rationale for stepped-up government involvement in inner cities.

Racism

At the core of offering a reversible "black-on-black violence" was presentation of an expedient notion: racism. This projected cause for "black-on-black violence" was something grim and debilitating of youth but also potentially changeable. It projected the reality of a racial prejudice in inner cities that damaged and afflicted kids but was confrontable and reversible. This notion, a key inclusion in the discourse, set up one central cause for this violence as a fruitful terrain for societal involvement. Racism, revealed as confrontable and eradicable, became a logical source for liberal intervention into inner cities. Notions of social improvement, to Murray Adelman (1988), must provide possibilities to reverse current situations. Offering this possibility, to Adelman, empowers suggestions of active intervention.

Columnists Leonita McClain (1982) of the *Chicago Tribune* and Larry Aubry (1987) of the *Los Angeles Sentinel* widely discussed racism in their renditions of black-on-black violence. Racism, first and foremost, was a psychic and social affliction on youth that contributed to black-on-black violence. Racism was pervasive ignorance and distrust of otherness steeped in misunderstanding that intensified anger and hopelessness in youth. As a process applied to black youth, its leading perpetrators— teachers, principals, school superintendents, other kids, city officials— attacked through labeling, stereotype, and denial of respect. To Larry Aubry (1987), this "wall of prejudice and racial discrimination remains substantially intact" today. While subtle, it communicated something devastating to youth: a sense of inferiority and unworthiness. Such actions, frequent and ritualized, intensified the problems of coping with poverty and social isolation that helped foster angry and discordant kids.

But while widespread, racism and black-on-black violence supposedly could be reversed. They could be swept away and were logical things to eradicate. But how this possibility was to be displayed was not a simple matter. Black youth as shown were represented as culturally devastated: they seemed hopelessly intransigent and hardly the lot to initiate cultural reversal. Many were supposedly all but culturally off the map, and their featuring in this reversal would be flagrantly hypocritical. At the same time, a general societal sense of who kids are (and who black kids are) militated against featuring this youth's agency. Kids, Mike Males (1997) notes, are widely seen as malleable and at-risk beings needing constant oversight. They, to Males, purportedly need stern guidance to avoid social problems: this need is even more the case for minority and poor youth.

In this context, liberals chose to focus on the racist-busting capacities of selected actors and institutions. They featured in discussions a network of tireless, streetwise, and racist-confronting advocates: social workers, reformed gang members, churches, advocacy ministers, and the courts. These advocates were activated in a text of caricatured figures associated with liberal presentations of "unfair cities": greedy landlords, hurt but resilient kids, needy but proud ghetto youth, and culturally off-the-map fathers. They boldly struck out across inner cities (more on this mental map in discourse in a moment) to confront racism. To the *Chicago Defender,* there are "valiant efforts of many African Americans who stubbornly continue to fight off . . . [racism]. Ex–gang members, according to the *Defender,* against terrible odds make interventions that remain marvels" (1988a, 9).

These liberal helpers toiled to provide equal opportunity for youth. They endlessly combed the recesses of black inner cities to do battle. In New York City and Detroit, as reported by *City Limits* writer Jill Kirschenbaum (1995), housing courts deftly read black inner cities and "routinely [gave] landlords with rap sheets as long as Pinocchio's nose the chance to make good faith efforts at repairs, no money down. . . . Countless trips downtown and years forced [landlords] to finally make repairs." In Chicago, said "black-on-black violence" activist Nancy Jefferson (1991), advocacy ministers "walked the streets and talked to kids about gangs, the streets, and what it took to overcome racism." They "spoke about alternative values and lifestyles that could stand up to racism and overcome it." Social workers, according to Jefferson, were "the eyes and ears for inner city equality" and helped "ease pain for kids." These liberal workers, in faithful and selfless spatial undertakings, unfailingly attended to a needy youth.

Of these benevolent institutions, churches received the most attention. These projected eyes and hearts of inner city streets strived to beat back racism in all its manifestations. The black inner city, a difficult world for black youth to navigate, was their anointed enemy. Local reporters, columnists, and politicians, again taking the lead, displayed these churches through the popular ethos of black religious advocacy (their emphasis on service and community) (see Osofsky 1966). This offering worked through the widespread public belief in dutiful, moral, and civic religious institutions. In Atlanta, for example, columnist Marcellus Harris (1991) of the *Atlanta Journal and Guide* declared inner city churches "dedicated to educating, empowering, and organizing . . . kids . . . for remedy and salvation." "Churches," said Harris, "seem so focused and determined to save [the] youth, as if the task was destined to be theirs." "The church," he said, was "the central figure in the pursuit for answers" about black-on-black violence.

Charismatic leaders were commonly featured in this offering of churches. Expeditions across inner city streets found them "talking the talk," "being profoundly moral," and "exuberantly revealing truth" (Indianapolis advocate Artura Chandler 1986). Interventions across barren and decrepit ghetto space illuminated tussling, courageous beings. Expansive visions digested youth habits and rituals, which were traced back to racism's influence. Their gazes easily read black inner cities as a prelude to action: Where racism was, and who was responsible for it, these leaders would decipher. Inner cities were now seeing increased church advocacy to stem black-on-black violence; these leaders were leading the charge. "In time," said the *Chicago Defender* (1988b), "the[se] grass roots heroes will ultimately conquer this [crime] problem, we cannot give up the struggle."

But making this liberal helper relied upon constituting and using a key mental space in narratives: "the struggled-through black inner city." This space was the thicket of physical and social ills that these warriors courageously engaged. Against this space, *New York Times* writer Rick Bragg's (1994) "barren, crumbling place[s]," heroic liberal salvationists could be seen. This space was made to rub against and make these salvationists as it did others in this narrating. Black kids bore its cultural and economic burdens, these advocates its possibilities for turnaround. Kids suffered in absorbing its ills, advocates flourished in confronting its ills. These advocates tirelessly engaged this space to combat racism. Everything liberals wanted these fighters to be—in values, spirit, vision—this locating in space helped provide.

We now know such space is activated by being made transparent. This maneuver characterized all mental spaces in the liberal as well as conservative discourses. But nowhere in the liberal discourse was making a process (racism) so dependent upon offering transparent spaces. For racism, unlike other objects offered, is commonly imagined as something slippery and elusive. As Julianne Malveaux (1993) points out, controversies have raged over racism's existence precisely because so many question its empirical existence. Mainstream America, to Malveaux, has tended to look for racism as obscured acts and concealed meanings that may reveal themselves only in refined and sophisticated glimpses onto the world. But under bold liberal strokes, racism was served up as something visible in space and readable. It was made something "out there" to be seen and immediately acted on.

But again classed and raced stereotypes permeated construction of one more black inner city figure. This construction of racist-busting church leaders, infused with liberal fantasy, belief, and salesmanship, was one more stereotyped being. These benevolent people, for all of their purported goodness, ultimately carried the stain of black primitiveness. This longstanding aspect of liberal renditions of activist blacks (see Mercer 1997) again served up cognitively superficial people. Thus, instead of being mental and ruminative like other racist confrontationalists (social workers, non–inner city politicians, city task force officials), they usually coarsely sensed and responded. For example, church leaders, according to Chicago advocate Nancy Jefferson (1991), were "in-motion organizers" with "sharp wits and instincts." *Atlanta Journal and Guide* columnist Marcellus Harris (1991) represented church leaders as "effervescent," "efficaciously energized," "enthusiastic," and offering "magnetic subject matter." Fighting racism, they ritually applied an instinctual acumen in classrooms, school board meetings, workplaces, and employment centers. Power to sense and react was their leading weapon.

With this making of racism, liberals seeded their "black-on-black violence" discourse with hope for fruitful change. Racism was made changeable and a cast of characters revealed as working for this change. While black youth appeared as passive subjects to racism, a host of progressive institutions fought to eradicate this passivity. Exposés of courage were sites to condense liberal theme. Through these sites, people could glimpse a rationale for public involvement in inner cities and for the people who should be leading the charge. But liberals never removed themselves from a hierarchical and custodial relation to their subjects: black youth and black communities. These kids and communities seemed all but incapable of self-uplift and needed external liberal involvement in their lives. Racism and violence could be addressed, but it required the resources of outside-liberal visions and strategies.

Black Political Leaders

"Black leaders" were another crucial object liberals constructed and seeded in the discourse to present possibility for reversing black-on-black violence. Elaborately narrating this figure was a logical choice: If the public was to see the potential for "black-on-black violence" turnaround, black leaders had to be rescued from criticisms by conservatives and many in the media of corruption and self-aggrandizement (see chapter 3). Liberals knew that many warily perceived these people (see Blount and Cunninghan 1996; Hill 1997). In response, liberals struck out to supplant this perception with equally simplified and unambiguous beings: benevolent and progressive leaders. Black leaders, made unswervingly righteous but in difficult circumstances, were another good-hearted agent working to help youth.

These leaders were made ideal for reclaiming black youth. An assigned character (instinctive, street-wise, able to talk the talk of youth) made them perfect confrontationalists. They supposedly knew these kids, knew the realities of black ghettos, and would sooner be pragmatic and tackle problems than waste time. Thus, to the *Cleveland Call & Post* (1994), a major voice on behalf of this politician, Cleveland's "Harliel Jones [a local black leader]" could "get right to the core of the problem, deal with these kids, and turn lives around." He "said the Black community must stop analyzing problems and start actively preserving solutions. . . . These solutions . . . include establishing self respect and not tolerating any elements in the community that are destroying it." With such leaders elaborated, in the discourse, society could feel relieved that these kids were being confronted.

But these leaders were surprisingly complex constructs. They, like other liberal salvationists, were a highly stylized construction that combined liberal sensibilities of humaneness, morality, and goodness with stereotypes of black politicians. On the one hand, as moral-liberal beings, they willingly traversed scary and barren turf to rescue and salvage kids. Where these gangs, drug-sellers, and at-risk youth were, these leaders would find them and struggle to help. The *Cleveland Call & Post* (1994), for example, frequently had this person locally and nationally combing ghettos to make a difference. Thus, "local Councilperson Harliel Jones exemplif[ied] that rare breed of leadership . . . by combining life experiences, street smarts, and philosophical integrity. . . . He . . . is a master of command and control. . . . When Jones speaks, people listen. What makes Jones's plea so powerful is not so much the message, but the messenger."

But this politician was frequently made one more stereotyped inner city being. "He" too was a projected artifact of black inner cities: in vision, allegiance, temperament, and personality. "He" was from this world and carried its character in him. The *Call & Post*'s Jones, in commentary, walked and talked repeatedly in the black community and "floated across city blocks" to spur change. Like other inner city black beings, he was raced and classed along mainstream middle-class lines. Liberals had him carrying an unshakable inner city blackness. Whatever he did, wherever he was, this ghettoscape stuck to him like glue. It could be ignored or disavowed, but typically permeated him. "He," not surprisingly, knew about the reality and pitfalls of drug addiction, gangs, and anti-societal values of youth.

Yet this offered black stereotype with liberal aesthetics produced an acceptable mainstream leader. It provided the sense of a progressive but conforming black leader. Thus, as strategic offering, mainstream America's thoughts and beliefs about these kids and communities were shared by these black leaders, for example, the core of the problem was values, the need to re-make underclass culture. These leaders accepted society's notion of devastated, different inner city kids. They too saw the problem as cultural and behavioral rather than structural or societal. So made, these leaders could be seen as acceptable extensions of mainstream desires. Both agreed on the problem and the solution; these leaders were situated in allegiance, mindset, and personality to spearhead a lifesaving, progressive intervention.

In this context, these leaders improvised and freelanced across inner cities with a purpose: to upgrade "their people." A mix of charisma, impromptu banter, and forceful confrontation propelled them. Placed before black audiences, their sense of duty to black youth was unshakable. Diverse ploys were used to engage kids: exhortations, recitations, threats, cajolement. Strategies sought to penetrate the typically rough exterior of kids that rampant cultural dysfunction cultivated. Here was the metaphor for tough love. Not surprisingly, these leaders saved their most impassioned strolls and orations for black children. For example, *Chicago Tribune* writers Dennis L. Buer and John Dzieken (1987) chronicle a youth interventionist, Dr. Carl Compton Bell, talking to kids at Chicago's St. Bartholomew church on the South Side. They write:

> [A]n explosion of noise welcomes Dr. Carl Compton Bell to the weekday Bible class . . . The rector, Darryl F. Jones, hushes the children and introduces his guest as a "fighter for the future of the black community. . . . Vaulting onto a stage in the church's basement, he begins to scrawl some grim numbers on a chalkboard, the sad facts of a pattern of violence among blacks that has made black-on-black murder a silent epidemic. [He] asks "Now, why are all these black men being murdered?" The answers come from around the room, from boys and girls: "Robbers" . . . "the devil" . . . "drugs" . . . "gangs" . . . "jail escapees". . . . "thieves" . . . "bad people." He cuts them short. "Y'all wrong" Bell says. "The answer is "us" and "guns." Bell, a forceful and charismatic presence, "looked them in the eye . . . and made them hear the truth." (Buer and Dzieken 1987, 23)

This constructing of black political leaders relied on making and setting them against a distinctive black inner city space, "politician confrontation space." In this setting, they were made incisive, in-motion interrogators of youth and communities that spilled across inner cities to talk of hope and possibility. In narrations, walks of these leaders typically flowed beyond traditionally safe terrain to take them to dangerous turf (gang blocks, dangerous streets, dilapidated neighborhoods). They, in the words of activist Nancy Jefferson (1991), "strolled confidently and purposely through acres of decline and preached compassion for law and order." Offering such spatial performance, to Tim Creswell (1996), is a time-tested discourse tactic to display benevolent people. It allows people to see a navigation of and confrontation with obstacles and ominous forces nestled across territories. In this setting, bold movements, gestures, and interrogations speak volumes. In cities, and particularly in inner cities, as Mike Presdee (2000) chronicles, this spotlighting becomes all the more powerful. Space is rendered a stage of spectacle and drama.

But this barren black ghettoscape was different from the other black inner cities mentioned: it was made unusually resistant to change. While other black inner cities used to narrate other things in the discourse often had children, kids, gangs, and families open to change, this one (the space to make black political leaders) less so. These differing resistance-to-change spaces were outgrowths of different identities being made. Other black inner cities in the discourse helped constitute churches, church leaders, outreach people, and social workers, people traditionally associated with hope and optimism. This one constituted black leaders, a more dubious figure in the public eye. Churches, church leaders, and the others were all about hope and were respected in common thought (see for example Higginbotham [1995, 1997] on churches and church leaders). Black leaders, in contrast, were commonly seen to wear multiple dubious identities: politicians, African Americans, and inner city beings.

One additional mental space, the blue-collar ideal, was at the heart of constructing these political leaders. This imaginary landscape, served up as a space of civilized values that these leaders professed allegiance to, helped endow these leaders with beliefs and goals that narrativists wanted them to have. This space in common thought, an icon of civility and normalcy, was the one that supposedly shaped their values and that they enthusiastically "wore." As one more human rendering to advance a liberal politics, this landscape of serene homes, ethnically cohesive streets, civil parks, and cleanliness was the well of values that purportedly infused these politicians. This space, as a kind of stand-in psychological profile, revealed the moral essence of these people. To know they wore this space, following Rob Shields, was to know their desires and goals.

Common thought, to Cameron McCarthy (1995), has this blue-collar space a world of tightly-knit ethnic groups allied to community and society. It has been assigned a host of virtuous values commonly associated with urban ethnic enclaves: pride in community, loyalty to family, commitment to the persistence of ethnic values, and desire to produce stalwart citizens. Its historical construction, made the authentic ethnic existence in cities, has timeless ethnic ways permeating it. Common presentations of the American Jewish, Irish, Polish, and Czech experience are examples. It, borrowing from Tim Creswell (1996), fits safely in the common imagining of a "law and order society." It falls comfortably within the domain of the "sensible" and "moderate" and thus has been used widely to infuse people with positive identities.

These leaders purportedly embodied and fought to reproduce this space. They routinely drew on it and sought to use it to communicate their character. It was Chicago politician Nancy Jefferson's (1991) "safe streets," "cheery blocks," "strong community allegiances," "strong family and home pride," "deep institutional affiliations," and "orderly streets and spaces." Black leaders, as Jefferson put it, "wanted to make Chicago's black community hardworking and tough in the face of adversity." These actions "reflected this politician's vision to put all people to work and have them commit to community upgrade." These leaders proudly advanced this upgrade vision: it fit with public perceptions of what they should be doing and were all about.

Why the liberal use of this blue-collar ideal? Because these were African Americans and politicians, and the suburban ideal was supposedly outside their imagining. In common thought, to Robin Kelley (1997), black urban leaders are widely seen as from "the world" of black inner cities and reflective of their values. In the liberal vision, to Robin Wagner-

Pacifici (1994), black politicians idealized have not been white politicians idealized. These are not just politicians, but black city politicians. Similarly, to Kelley, "black inner cities" are commonly viewed as spaces that in upgrade look to achieve "the utopian ethnic condition": social stability in an ethnically conscious, blue-collar harmony. This was what these racial activists set in inner cities purportedly desired and were trying to create. Liberals, in making this leader, did not escape the deeply rooted stereotypes of blacks previously discussed. But with black leaders endowed with these positive attributes, why the history of failed performance? Black leaders, as seen by liberals like Rosalind Rossi (1981) of the *Chicago Sun-Times*, worked through enormously difficult circumstances. As discussed, liberals offered economic and social indicators and stark mappings of black inner city social geographies that demonstrated ravaged spaces. Families were disappearing, people hustled often through illegal means to survive, many lost trust in the system and themselves, and kids were becoming dysfunctional. In this difficult context, leaders were projected to be able to do only so much. To S. Harris (1994) of the *Akron-Beacon Journal,* "they can't do anything [substantial] because it's the people on the streets who need to learn to talk things through instead of shooting it out." Black politicians, according to Harris, fought courageously and maneuvered boldly across inner cities but often with limited successes.

At the same time, these liberals placed black leaders within tough cultural constraints. To writer Usani Perkins (1991), black leaders had to navigate worlds hostile to African Americans—rules, styles of conduct, cultural codes, power configurations—to secure legitimacy and resources. On the one hand, as Perkins pointed out, they had to play this world's games—"talk the talk, walk the walk"—to be authenticated and secure resources. To be too extreme or haughty was to risk punishment in the form of diminished resources. In playing this game, according to Perkins, black leaders could sometimes seem "white": appearing overly adjustive to white society. And occasionally white society's carrots were enticing and corrupting. But black leaders usually stayed righteous and rarely lost commitment to black communities.

Black Culture

A final key discourse object to seed hope and possibility for "black-on-black violence" turnaround was black culture. This object is perhaps surprising given the now documented notion of "black inner city" cultural decline. "Black culture" as discussed (also commonly termed "underclass culture," "ghetto subculture," "black subculture" by these narrativists) was offered as a central cause for black-on-black violence. This deteriorating glue of values and morals, a crucial communicative element in the discourse, seared residents in a context of deepening poverty and disenfranchisement. These youth and spaces, purportedly decimated by this culture, were profoundly damaged.

But establishing possibilities for youth change in discourse, following Murray Adelman (1988), requires advancing a sense of cultural renewal. Culture, to Adelman, is widely seen as something that empowers youth. Youth purportedly become through culture: they embody it, act on it, and transmit it. Culture supposedly promotes or obstructs progress: people become enduring testimonials to its virtues and defects. Thus liberals presented a culture construct that was currently deficient but also a potentially fertile source of black community enrichment. Deformed norms and values could be transformed should anyone, in the words of the *Cleveland Call & Post* (1992), "work to address the growing human toll of 'black-on-black violence.'" This germ of destruction could be reversed; it could be made nurturing and fruitful.

But liberals less confidently displayed this potential of "black culture." They richly depicted decrepit worlds but groped to "reveal" black culture's unlocked possibilities. Paraphrasing Cora Kaplan (1996), condemning subjects to a cultural captivity made displaying cultural prospects difficult. In this context, black culture as potential found expression in sketches of a culture's two parts, a people's aesthetic attributes (distinctive arts, lifestyles, sense of self, sense of pride) and core values (drive to assimilate, allegiance to being productive citizens as waged and community workers, efficacy of individualism). These two parts, properly cultivated, could create Indianapolis councilman Glen Howard's (1987) "proud, heritage-rich Black American." This being "would stabilize black communities . . . and keep these areas rich and vigorous."

This black cultural potential celebrated black difference but as something tied to social sameness. Sense of distinctiveness about "a people" combined with established economic and political beliefs in the mainstream to constitute a black cultural ideal. This culture concept, with its two parts, thus endowed African Americans with a mission: to distinguish themselves aesthetically while embracing mainstream market-based ideals. To paraphrase Robin Kelley (1997), there were to be "black ways" of doing things but these were to be bounded by accepting norms of a hyper-market-based society. Cultivating a creative and distinctive aesthetics had to meld with an established sense of responsible and upstanding citizens. If this black culture could be made across black communities, and kids widely responded to it, in the discourse black-on-black violence would greatly diminish.

But making and communicating this cultural potential notion hinged on presentation of a key mental space: the "once culturally cohesive black ghettoscape." This was an idealized space of a once glorious black community that displayed icons of black cultural coherence, that proclaimed this community's once true authenticity. What progressive black culture could create in the current black community, it was said, this space was. Integrated into discussions of black community prospects and possibilities, it illuminated what black inner cities could be. This space was thus used as the visible evidence of positive black culture at one time upholding black communities; harmony and serenity were everywhere across it. Black cultural potential, in this sense, was invoked both graphically and in language. If black culture had created such a neighborhood once, it was suggested, black culture could do it again.

This space invoked haunting spatial images. It contained icons of black cultural coherence—families mingling on stoops on warm summer evenings, orderly parks monitored by mothers and fathers, neat and tidy houses, bustling and safe streets—in a community setting. This community was assiduously watched and monitored. Streets and parks were vibrant, clean, and safe. People gathered on stoops on summer evenings to mingle, gossip, and play. Stores and taverns stayed open late as elements integrated into the community's fabric. And friendly cops were omnipresent. As Lorraine Miller in the *New York Amsterdam News* (1989) describes, "Do you remember when every street corner had a familiar figure dressed in a blue uniform? In my neighborhood, it was Denny the cop. He knew each of the kids by name and he looked after us. . . . [and] everyone reading this column can surely remember when children could play their games in front of their houses or ride their bicycles or walk to school without another's concern."

To bolster a sense of possibility for cultural turnaround, many liberals also sketched another mental space: improved black inner cities. This "space of cultural rebirth" was a terrain that displayed the beginning of positive community change. Set in the themes of the discourse previously discussed, it was a glaring paradox. Now downgraded lives and spaces (see first half of this chapter) were supplanted by engaging youth, vacant lots being monitored by families, and mothers busily strolling to markets and neighbors' homes. This upbeat and constructive space encoded one of the discourse's deepest moral drives: to display possibilities for youth and community upgrade. Thus a leading liberal voice chronicling this cartographics in Indianapolis, *Star* writer Rob Schneider (1987), notes: "The black community is showing the signs of change . . . The streets are being freed up in a slow reversal of community change . . . stores are staying open . . . the elderly are feeling more confident to walk." "The streets are still a tough and uncertain place," Schneider adds, "but sense of possibility for renewal and full-fledged recapture is in the air."

Unlike before, kids, mothers, institutional heads, and people had vision. They had eyes, could see problems in community, and could begin to move forward. In this context, numerous agents set in this "improving black community" were activated to nurture black culture. Churches were again featured to energetically "work ghetto neighborhoods" in bold interventions. They preached a resonant morality and set of values. To syndicated columnist Monique Parsons (1999, 6), "the black church is one of the oldest living institutions in the nation, and it is the oldest institution that black Americans truly call their own." Their mission was to "face . . . crises head-on . . . poverty, crime, drug abuse, unemployment, rising teen-age pregnancy rates, the breakdown of the traditional family and rising incarceration rates for young black men." Parsons' churches deftly maneuvered across black communities. Their leaders didn't just stay home and preach in the pulpit, they were out engaging kids.

This space in the discourse was strategic: it communicated the possibility for black inner city turnaround. Its luminous images signaled that these neighborhoods could be positively changed. This space mobilized the imagining of possibility. In the process, seeing unveiled the potential for progressive and fruitful liberal intervention in inner cities. Sight became a liberal political tool that enabled their political agenda. These neighborhoods could be salvaged; this space was proof. What remained to be done was to mobilize resources and strategies and turn black inner cities around. As sight showed, the tide was already turning; resolve was necessary.

In this context, church leaders spoke of black culture and "black-on-black violence" as reversible. The need was for Dr. Louis Sullivan's "culture of character" to upgrade kids and eradicate this violence (in *New York Times* 1994). Liberals voiced a kind of *Geist* in black inner cities that never died amid a decline and perversion of culture. As destructive values and beliefs became widespread and normal in inner cities, a deep reservoir of past ways held on in the crevices of black inner city life. "Civility never perished in the ghetto," according to Indianapolis councilman Glen Howard (1987); "[w]e had already flowered in a civility of our own making, we needed to recapture this and its constructive spirit." To the *Chicago Defender* (1988a), "generations of Blacks . . . were able to build great edifices; obtain education against terrible odds; make inventions that remain marvels of the world." Such ingenuity, according to the *Chicago Defender,* needed to be meticulously cultivated if black-on-black violence were to be reduced.

The Final Product

This chapter suggests that this liberal discourse, like its conservative counterpart, comprised both a "field of understanding" and direct statements about a "black-on-black violence" construct that meshed imperceptibly. Each of these depended upon the other for content and foundation. In totality, they validated one confining vision of this violence set inside a storehouse of self-evident truths. The field of understanding was this violence's validating setup that provided these direct statements with coherence and support. It was the truth about people, places, and processes involved in this violence. But as a human intervention ("narration") onto a complex world, it was truth from one political perspective steeped in interpretation, belief, values, and the spurning of alternatives. The public was offered one rendition of violence whose coherence ultimately depended upon a slick imposing of presences, absences, and discursive backdrop.

Space helped build this discourse and was used, most importantly, as "representations of space." This space as imagined landscapes in discourse provided meanings and content to the staged reality of the black inner city and direct discussions of this violence. It "shot through" renditions of diverse people, processes, and places as a kind of framing resource, adding an imagined visibility and order to scripted characteristics and attributes of these. These spaces interwoven in the discourse were as fundamental to building this reality of "black-on-black violence" as any ploy or resource used. Its "fabric" was a tool to advance liberal politics as a frequently taken-for-granted resource. Widely seen as passive and harmless, this space gave form and meaning to the discourse.

Through use of space the discourse communicated this violence in four phases: social breach, crisis, need for response, and hope for reintegration. Social breach displayed a tear in cultures across inner city America that interrupted smoothly-functioning life. Once-healthy values in black inner cities were disintegrating in a spiral of decline. Increased numbers of black youth had veered out of control; many opposed mainstream values. Crisis showed a heinous result of this cultural tear: the rise of "black-on-black violence." Black inner cities were the new killing fields, with victims and residents huddling in sheer terror. A cast of characters fleshed out the script: ferocious youth, hustling pimps, savvy prostitutes, toiling mothers, dandyish men, hardened hustlers, struggling social workers, and deadened teachers.

Need to respond built from the previous two stages and identified best solutions. Government involvement was a potentially dramatic and courageous stroke that could resuscitate kids and communities. Society had to recenter these kids in the mainstream by reengineering failing and defective cultures (more policing, more efficient local courts, job creation, job training, more school aid). Kids and neighborhoods had severely eroded but reversal was still possible. The final stage was hope for reintegration, the outcome of progressive policy. Liberals implored the public to support their initiatives or these people and places would be completely lost. Liberal initiatives were made the last and best hope for a floundering people and place. Conservative prescription, in contrast, would deepen depravity.

Liberals and conservatives ultimately shared key similarities in visions of this violence. At the core, both offered one dominant and haunting image in discourse: the roaming pathological youth. This counter-societal and impulsive kid communicated that local culture always grounded youth. This dominating presence packed with signifiers (dress, body movement, facial expression) reinforced dimly acknowledged "truths" in mainstream America: inner city blacks were one category of people, culture propelled human actions, culture seamlessly guided kids, and "black-on-black violence" was rooted in cultural dysfunction. These "truths" (Bourdieu's habitus) made the liberal "leading" with culture powerful. Like conservative renditions, the liberal discourse reinforced that powerful culture was a timeless reality that was fundamental to explaining actions of youth.

In this context, references to contextual societal forces crashed. This content was blunted by failure to control the dominating imagery of culturally imploding inner cities and youth. Offerings of contextual forces, perhaps unsurprisingly, barely resonated after a while even with many liberals, who through the 1980s increasingly dived into the wickedly delicious dissection of black youth and black inner cities. This engagement, in full color and costume, snowballed with a sense of its own melodrama and histrionics. These liberals increasingly fell victim to their own passion to illuminate ghastliness, intensifying their scripting of tragic morass that communicated the power of local culture and human agency all too clearly.

5

Communicative Similarities in Discourse

This chapter compares the characteristics of the discourses just discussed to deepen our understanding of how this dominant vision of violence ("black–on–black violence") formed in public thought. This discussion is important. We now know that both discourses richly narrated a problem notion of culture in order to explain this violence; it was provided elaborate detail and embellishment. These narrations fit with established mainstream understandings of inner city "realities," that is, what inner city social life was like, what kind of people dwelled here, and what kids here were like. These discourses, in this sense, effectively extended the past into the present. This solid interconnection of history with the current was potent. The present, in the process, was "shot through" with the past to form a seamless historical continuum.

But this chapter chronicles that this communication of a causal, problem culture involved more than a simple identifying and embellishing. Here I document the importance of two other communicative processes in the discourses: the theatrical style of presentation and the image-laden concepts used by both groups. The liberal discourse, the focus, was most importantly guilty of these, which unified its base of meanings with the conservative discourse. These two communicative processes, I suggest, were critical communicative structures that helped liberal discussions bolster conservative assertion. I therefore suggest that style of presentation as shown by these two processes was also at the heart of what the discourses transmitted. It was not merely what they said but how they said it that functioned as important communicative process. Set in unusually conservative times, the Reagan years and beyond, one dominant way of seeing this issue emerged.

Style of presentation and choice of language were obvious dimensions in the liberal discourse but less obviously communicated the causative influence of culture. These two processes, I suggest, potently communicated in nearly taken-for-granted ways. First, theatricalizing kids and their worlds offered eye-popping and ghastly items that reinforced the influence of "cultural things." As people commonly imagined culture to be and to operate in inner cities, it was served up to them in deliciously wicked terms. Cultural things in common consciousness—clothes, gaits, facial expressions, lifestyles, patterns of consumption—resonated in image to communicate a sense of cultural group: "underclass blacks." Second, this violence was spoken through terms already colonized in image and meaning by conservatives. These post–1980 liberals, ultimately, drew on terms that carried potent conservative meanings to communicate inadvertently about people, places, and processes.

A final brief introductory point. I reiterate that it is fruitless to divorce these processes of communication (and the discourse statements that flagrantly asserted a problem culture) from a history of society's constructing the importance of culture in black life. A glib usage of a William Faulkner adage is appropriate: "the past is not dead; it's not even past." The post–1980 vision of "black-on-black violence" was a discourse that invoked the power of local culture in a historical continuum. This "black-on-black violence" was a rendition of the present that extended past beliefs about culture's power in local affairs. It crystallized in the national consciousness, but only with discourse deftly connecting to the past. This power of history, as chapter 2 detailed, should never be forgotten.

Communicating Culture: People and Place as Spectacle

It is now known that the ploy of spectacle these liberals used can be an influential textual maneuver. Sensibilities to things (people and processes) are heightened with presentation of fantastic and eye-popping detail. Like no other stylistic ploy, subjects are pushed into the realm of the unique and theatrical. The process of spectacle, to Walkowitz (1992), offers outlandishness, with viewers taken to difference, otherness, and the fantastic. Such "disclosure" taps a deeply established sense of norms to reveal the spectacle of their antitheses: the strikingly appealing, devastatingly beautiful, garishly offensive, hideously destructive, remarkably appalling. This material of the spectacle is often the stuff, not surprisingly, for producing moral panics, unfolding controversies, perplexing issues, trenchant anxieties, and darkest fears.

Yet spectacle can serve other political purposes besides highlighting non-normative people and places. Nothing inherent in spectacle makes this an automatic device for impugning. In fact, spectacle has been widely used across time to mock established understandings in common thought. In medieval Europe, as Bakhtin (1981) demonstrates, enactment of spectacle was often a deeply subversive act, a communicating through caricature and grotesqueness that ridiculed status quo cultural categories and their supposed naturalness. Players used costume and body movements to center and lampoon common belief. The strategy, according to Bakhtin, was to show an alternative truth through critique of common assumptions that "reduced lie[s] to absurdit[ies]." This is Wagner-Pacifici's (1994) "restor[ing] truth through the back door" that makes visible and criticizes established assumptions.

Spectacle in this sense is like language, a hollow vessel that gets filled with intentions and drives. It can be mobilized in the service of many kinds of politics. Like use of space, spectacle plays with realities and can be subversive or status quo. But spectacle more often than not protects status quo conditions and relations and has an enormous capacity to wield oppression. In the process, it can help make and sustain sense of problem identities, deformed places, cancerous processes, and defective institutions that restrict spatial mobility, economic advancement, and serious political engagement with prevailing power. In making or upholding "regimes of truth," its repercussions can be profound. Seemingly innocuous spectacle used this way, then, offers a reality and criticizes alternatives. Spectacle this way communicates a reality but also "speaks" about the delusions of alternatives.

Spectacle can be staged in numerous forms (physically, textually). Fairs, marches, demonstrations, celebrations, and architectural inscriptions are its physical forms, narrations of people and places its textual versions. Such spectacle, in more than one of these forms, typically surrounds people in daily life. One is sometimes aware of spectacle; many times one is not. It permeates life in ways we take for granted and in rituals of declaration. Tim Creswell (1996) sees spectacle in urban rioting, Mikhael Bakhtin (1981) in ritualized carnival, David Harvey (1989) in architecture, Robin Wagner-Pacifici (1994) in public pronouncement. The power of words, built urban form, and concentrations of people (festivals, concerts), to these theorists, are prime sites for this staging.

When spectacle reinforces established understandings of people, places, and processes, it typically unmasks things social consensus already knows or suspects. For example, in contemporary society, to Harvey, spectacle is found in among other things postmodern architecture. Its sense of surface glitter, transitory participatory pleasure, and ephemerality poke fun at modernist styles but also celebrate status quo kinds of restructuring and downtown redevelopment. This glitzy architecture (supplanting austere modernism) communicates in a new way established cultural and economic understandings about cities (downtown as cultural jewel, downtown as home for elite, expressive aesthetics). An age-old politics is affirmed: cities are to be transformed to meet changing economic and corporate circumstances. Needs of business and conspicuous consumers should continue to be paramount: they are the economic engine of cities. To Harvey, a new kind of architecture, advertising pastiche and glitter, sustains sense of timeless capitalist truths.

Alternatively, subversive spectacle unmasks established assumptions and values. It reveals through sensation and caricature alternative views of people, places, and processes. Caricature becomes commentary that projects new ways to see and think. This kind of spectacle, like the previous, can be influential politics. Use of caricature, in this sense, provides "spaces" for people to use and mobilize. Peter Jackson (1988) finds this kind of spectacle in the Caribbean carnival. A yearly assemblage of floats and reverie allows disenfranchised people to dwell in and contemplate difference in a world of caricature. The poor offer renditions of the oppressive state and local capital that contest established understandings. Such practices, in the process, open up opportunities to engage alternative realities and possibilities.

But spectacle that reinforces established understandings of people, places, and processes is more common and marks many discourses (including the ones this book engages). Yet such spectacle cannot avoid being revealing sites of meaning about its makers. Like Barthes's (1972) masks, these are "locations" where narrativists display their values. Glimpsing them is to see projection of moral centers, peripheries, ideals, and norms. The spectacle shows narrativist desires and values for all to see. It illuminates what narrativists have decided is threatening, peculiar, devious, onerous, troublesome, normative, custom, and tradition. The spectacle, like Richard Rorty's mirror, reflects back to observers society's hierarchy. To know dominant social assertions, Mikhael Bakhtin (1981) notes, one only has to study its presentation of spectacle.

This chapter's focus, these post-1980 liberals, obsessively theatricalized "inner city black youth" and "black inner cities" in a manner that reinforced established mainstream understandings. The dilemma was the unrealized power of spectacle to communicate the influence of agency and culture. Here was a kind of "sub-communicating" that inadvertently spoke to the sense of the "true and real." Its invoking reinforced stereotype and established understandings of their central subject matter—violent black kids—as it dragged along chains of signifiers: notion of culture as sets of values embedded in neighborhoods, culture as driving force behind the actions of youth, this youth as carrier of cultural content, and these kids as now atrociously non-normal. Every time the spectacle of roaming black youth appeared, it carried with it these chains of association. This offered spectacle, borrowing from Henri Lefebvre (1984), always spotlighted and passed judgment on people, settings, and processes. It invoked fantastic acts of individuals that asked people to "call up" and fall back on established understandings of a people and their communities.

Spectacle, Mike Presdee (2000) notes, can be a license to transgress; that is what these liberals accomplished by using it. But, paradoxically, it transgressed against themselves. As liberals, their words and phrases spoke of troubled and hurt people; their spectacle of life and crime said otherwise. Here was the collision of ambivalence par excellence. Words and phrases outlined societally afflicted kids, but spectacle communicated audaciously bad decision-making of culturally abhorrent youth. Numerous analysts, particularly Michael Burawoy (1979), have discussed the problems writers and speakers encounter as they use strategies to rivet attention on constructs (people and processes). "Texts," to Burawoy, can decisively "speak" against themselves in subterranean ways. This was the trap these liberals fell into.

But having said this, I also suggest at this point that things were not quite this simple. At the same time, I believe, some liberals were far from innocent in continuously invoking this spectacle. For some, this ploy inadvertently boomeranged as a communicative device to disrupt their structural argument. This is the notion I have advanced to this point. But for other liberals, offer of spectacle afforded opportunity to participate in a kind of deeper, real communicating. I suggest spectacle was used for different purposes among these particular liberals, always being the preferred ploy to sensationalize this youth and their setting, but among some, a way to truly speak their truths. Let me explain.

On the one hand, these liberals were supposed to place black youth and black spaces in the realm of fantastically disadvantaged and societally afflicted. This "sobriety of the normative" (Presdee 2000) involved liberals "acting out" roles and rules. Post-1980 liberals discussing inner cities were to see a startling fall into decline and poverty. But offer of spectacle also provided opportunity for some to move beyond roles and rules and to communicate their dissatisfaction about black youth and community. It was not a clear and coherent dissatisfaction but instead, borrowing from Allen Pred (1984), "a trace of feeling" at the center of liberal ambivalence about these kids. This trace, as documented in chapter 4, also took the form in discourse of liberals periodically speaking of irresponsible youth choices for black-on-black violence in a very uncertain articulation.

In sum, this making of spectacle was rooted in the drive to show a grim black youth situation. "Revealing" horror and atrocity was central to liberals' conveying their concern about human suffering and the need for help. But to reduce construction of spectacle to this in all cases among all of these narrativists is naïve. I suggest that it also served, as a subsidiary to a greater cause, to communicate their barely-able-to-be-acknowledged "reality" of irresponsible youth. These were, after all, to these liberals, kids that violated their sensibilities: they were seen to reject societal norms and flaunt their differences from the societal mainstream.

They often flagrantly performed a vile and senseless act, taking life, with little remorse. These bothered liberals as acts that spurned liberal beliefs about community and communality. These liberals, too, were angry about these acts, and in exposés of forces and faces in inner cities perceived mainly the appearance of hostility and intransigence.

In this context, the offer of spectacle was elaborate. Liberals highlighted staggering and stubborn kids and families even as benevolent institutions and politicians were made to hustle around. Their "reality" was war zones complete with battles, casualties, leaders, foot soldiers, and spaces of social disorganization. People reeled from economic and cultural devastation; everyday survival was a day-to-day proposition. People huddled in sheer terror to avoid escalating violence. Outrageously struggling and lost kids in garish settings were aggressors in an ongoing war between two parties: constructive versus destructive cultural bearers. These staged sites were outrageously frantic, dangerous, and unpredictable. As frenetic people danced through and around dysfunction like minefields ready to explode, life went on.

At the core of this scene was the hulking black youth that invoked frightening power and daunting strength. "He" was the strong and resilient thing that lurked in the shadows. "His" game—drugs, women, violence, intimidation, and gangs—as garish and compelling. Boldly stepping forth at a moment's notice, he could in an instant fall back into the teeming mass of inner city black bodies. Obvious one moment and concealed in the next, "he" was a repugnant yet fascinating character. "His" walk, less a stroll than a marauding prowl, spurned sense of rationality; he was capable of doing anything. His unpredictability could result in confrontation, conflict, violence, and death. A discord and impulsiveness pulsated across inner cities; the theater of black kids in these spaces was incendiary.

This staging of spectacle also spotlighted another icon of troubled inner city youth, the ominous freewheeling gang. Gangs were served up as bodies without heads set on paths of violence and destruction. As outgrowths of pathological families and neighborhoods, they navigated urban terrain through a brute physicality. It was the scariest kind of physicality—impulsive, whimsical, deadly—that made them fearless and feared. These surly and uncompromising apostles of violence barely reasoned and comprehended. As primitive and remorseless creatures, they seemed to stand outside civility's constructive engagement. What "they" understood and respected through their subculture was what common civility so sharply shunned: force, brute strength, and decisive retaliation.

These liberals also forged fantastically scarred black inner cities. Once proud and morally grounded, these places were being overrun by an insidious street culture. This culture's lethal effects purportedly sapped thinking, prowess, and hope. No corner of community seemed able to escape the culture's devastating ravaging. Black inner cities were marked as so fantastically isolated from worth and prestige—producers of goods and services, moral steadfastness, civic pride, selfless nurturers of youth—that they became bearers of the empty and insignificant. Nearly spent block clubs, churches, tenant groups, and neighborhood watches were the last bastions of civility that stood toe to toe against escalating menaces. The battlegrounds for the inner city's soul were streets, playgrounds, parks, schools, and common thought. Blunt exposés took the public to fantastically failing places that spotlighted aspiration-blunted and disoriented people wandering through chaotic worlds. The sensational was found everywhere; the amazingly scarred had become ritual and routine.

But there was more to this application of spectacle that needs to be discussed. While these liberals engaged in portrayal of "the objective reality of spectacle" that has just been chronicled, they also used spectacle as a theme to help make the identity of black youth. Here they injected this ploy into the documented goals and ambitions of kids as they narrated them. This liberal use of spectacle, in other words, took two forms. The first, already discussed, illuminated an "everyday ghetto spectacle" where common life in black ghettos was made a spectacular stage. But at the same time, another use of spectacle, a "behavioral spectacle," involved coding kids as in hot pursuit of theater and drama that defined and displayed their identities. This use coded these kids as youth on the move who could only be satiated by participating in the fantastically abhorrent. Let me explain.

These liberals richly depicted this new black youth as madly in pursuit of spectacle on a daily basis. Such acts as "wilding" and "gang-banging," liberals communicated, provided excitement and a dramatic break from the boredom of being wageless and wealthless in a consumer society. This was a slightly more humane use of spectacle, but barely. Hurt and suffering kids found a carnivalesque kind of recreational outlet in being transgressive and violent. Instead of racing hot cars or derisively cutting classes like their suburban counterparts, they joyously intimidated others, seized turf, broke bones, or killed. These were the supposedly new, sanctioned ways to relieve the ennui of ghetto life. To liberals, this pursuit of spectacle was always perverse and celebrated new ways to strike out against societal norms.

Roaming gangs and the violence they brandished were a featured element. Their actions were offered as elaborate turf wars that pockmarked inner cities. At one level, this was made a kind of territorial behavior. Black kids in gangs acted instinctively to appropriate turf and to expand their sphere of influence. But it was also offered as a spatial conquest that celebrated a sense of accomplishment. These performances required intimidative, insinuative, and tactical skills. This violence was made one part of a "carnival of conflict" that excited and affirmed. These streets were contests over the symbolic. To take control of this public domain was to claim a kind of ownership that elaborated identity, communal display, and accomplishment.

The carnival of conflict danced up and down the streets of inner cities. Emboldened kids confronted and assaulted in a performative aggression. To take someone out randomly and indiscriminately was an exalting flaunting of counter-societal values. In these lives, violence was a kind of theater whose unpredictability (who would be "taken out?" would there be a scuffle? could the act occur cleanly? would the assaulting kid get caught?) was exciting. Against the boredom of constricted inner city life, this symbolic violence was expressive and dramatic. Nothing else could fit the bill; everyday life had degenerated into hyperaggressive theater. Befitting this staging, kids were "dressed" and "bodied" as participants in the carnival of violence. The accoutrements of garish celebrants marked their appearance: earrings, baggy and sagging pants, tilted baseball caps, hip-hop sneakers, strong bodies, defiant gazes, and taut legs.

Displaying the youth pursuit of spectacle to constitute their identities has a long history in academic and journalistic writing. Liberals, in this sense, borrowed from a rich literary tradition, one that is politically diverse and not confined to cultural liberalism. A vivid illustration is Mike Presdee's recent analysis (2000) of the carnival of crime in the United Kingdom. In 1991 and 1992, according to Presdee (who rejects cultural liberalism), a number of cities throughout Britain were thrust into the limelight as sites for car theft and ritualized joyriding. In one part of Oxford, the Blackbird Leys Housing Estate, this theft of autos was unusually pronounced. This area suffered from high unemployment, relative poverty, and racial tension. Closure of the Cowley car plant in 1992 intensified these conditions.

Under the shadow of the car factory, a culture of cars helped make car theft a celebratory act. Skills to steal a car, which car to steal, how to gain entry, and how to illegally start an engine rendered this a spectacular and accomplished undertaking. In this context, joyriding became celebration of a form of car culture that was carnivalesque, performance-centered, and criminal. The sport of joyriding involved teams of youths spotting a "hatch," stealing it, and delivering it to a driver. In the evenings, the cars would be raced around the estate to show off skill. Cars, in the words of Presdee, were both the first and the second life of the estate. In the first life, they created them and in the second life celebrated and destroyed them.

Why is this use of spectacle important to our analysis? Because its use in the discourse reinforced the sense of a culturally lost, compensating participant in black-on-black violence. Like conservative renditions, these kids were communicated as profoundly fallen into a cultural wilderness. These were not kids struggling to be socially and morally the same, but damaged youth who now rejoiced in being in another world. The multiple uses of spectacle worked in tandem to reinforce this perception. These uses displayed remarkably different kids in different worlds, irresponsible choosers of life paths and lifestyles, and kids in hot pursuit of the carnival of violence. The final use of spectacle, revealing rational and goal-seeking kids, was "platformed" by the former use. In this context, questions raised about this youth were troubling: What kind of kids would find recreation in violence? What kind of a social fabric would make such actions normal? Who were these kids that reveled in the symbolism of someone shot or stabbed?

Subverting Terms

But another process in this liberal communicating helped unify their conveyed content with conservatives: use of terms. In this section I demonstrate that this use unleashed trapped meanings built up in terms over time
that communicated above and beyond liberal dictates. Key terms, I suggest, were profoundly the property of America's conservative heritage.
Unknown to many of these liberals, the language of cities and civil society in the 1980s (ghettos, slums, underclass neighborhoods, black poor,
culture, underclass culture) was a complex storehouse for meanings.
These concepts, momentarily borrowed and worked through to communicate liberal truths, were colonized property that imperceptibly pushed
historical understandings of people and processes into the present.

What was at work here? These concepts, I suggest, dragged complex
histories with them every time they were used. They were evolving storehouses for the interplay between past and present understanding of people, places, and processes. These concepts, following Mikhail Bakhtin
(1981), were involved in an uninterrupted historical becoming that char-
acterizes all language. Meanings seared into them carried past and current
content that melded with each other. To extract meanings from these
terms was to "pull from them" historically constructed and updated understandings. This insight has been noted by numerous prominent writers
about language. For example:

> Language is present to the novelist only as something stratified and
> heteroglot . . . Each word tastes of the context and contexts in which it
> has lived its socially charged life; all words and forms are populated by
> intentions. (Bakhtin 1981, 293)

> My voice gives the illusion of unity to what I say; I am, in fact, con-
> stantly expressing a plenitude of meanings, some intended, others of
> which I am unaware. (Hulquist 1981, xx)

> Language becomes the depository of a large aggregate of collective
> sedimentations . . . [it] builds up semantic fields or zones of meaning
> that are linguistically circumscribed. (Berger and Luchmann 1966, 41)

This process was crucial in the liberal discourse: a paradox was that liberals failed to unify meanings in terms with contextual themes for "black-on-black violence." Liberals spoke of societal and contextual influences on this youth, but meanings in terms said otherwise. Without unification, each "sphere" jumped out as a different domain of communication. Two streams of meanings (among others), terminologically laden ones and thematic-contextual ones, clashed in liberal pronouncements in a battle of realities and causes. The first stream, terminologically laden meanings, was the incrementally constructed content welled up in terms over decades: the essence of inner city black kids, mothers, families, men, and institutions. The second, thematic-contextual meanings, were ideas in the "black-on-black violence" discourse about societal forces: deindustrialization, plant closures, spatial mismatch of workers to jobs, and societal racism.

In this battle the meanings that triumphed had no contest. Meanings in terms encompassed a wealth of intuitive understandings; those from contextual themes did not. One set of meanings was grounded and instinctive, the other less so. In being less intuitive, they were capable of being understood by readers but less amenable to being taken as factual and causal. To Jay Lemke (1995), discussions of structural and societal forces unsupported by "the power of terms" often fail to resonate with people. Two "worlds" of meanings are unfurled that pit one against the other. Meanings in terms, to Lemke, can be master subverters of thematic content. Without engagement by narrativists, these meanings will insinuate themselves into current constructions of understanding. Such meanings, to Lemke, can be eradicated or can spill into current understanding depending upon narrativist treatment of terms. To deeply examine terms is to open up possibilities to recode them and to have these recodings coincide with thematic content. But to assume neutrality of terms or easy counter-usage is to fall victim to the politics of "the word."

These liberals, I believe, worked from a common misunderstanding: Ideas and politics turn on simple use of language. Working through and tinkering with language, they failed to understand its deepest workings. They sought to rework concepts to yield distinctive understandings. But this reworking did not purge terms of their deep meanings and content (more on the specific terms in a moment). Terms reflected complex and persistent systems of domination; elaborate hierarchies were written into them. Meanings in terms, not easily removed, stuck to what Bakhtin (1981) calls the archive of these. Terms, to Bakhtin, always exude the essence of their "lived," charged lives and swell with intentions. Terms do not submit easily to change, resisting assimilation into thematic message that can confound intent of discourses.

Examining precise terms shows this: let me focus on two terms consistently used. The first, the term "black family," was frequently invoked but was a luminous conservative concept (see chapter 3). Liberals strived to code this term as a garishly different, struggling, and wounded element in black inner cities. This offering helped display "the new 1980s inner city decline" as a vivid reflection of a now grotesquely different ghetto life. Discussion tied this notion to both structure and agency: punishing deindustrialization, degenerating culture, spatial mismatch, a new service-oriented economy, lingering racism, and bad individual decision-making. This family was a critical facet of the field of understanding through which "black-on-black violence" was to be known.

But negative content filled this term as a taut, entrenched set of meanings. As Cameron McCarthy (1995) reveals, common thought imaged these families as imploding units dwelling in chaotic settings. History placed in this term communicated a sense of dysfunctional social unit as leading edge of a massive social tear in inner cities. For example, as my interviews in Chicago and Indianapolis bore out, this family was commonly associated with "angry young mothers," "combustible people," "rebellious and troubled kids," and "irresponsible and hedonistic fathers" (LaBaj 1986; Ben West 1987). Black families were widely seen as troubled and troubling things. "Black families" in America had become a condensed site for inner city cultural ills in the 1980s; liberals failed to purge these meanings. A truly progressive vision of this family, I suggest, would have offered more than compassionate understanding for their plight and thin recitals of societal influences on them.

What was the history stored in this term? Much evidence suggests that "the black family" appeared as a full-blown problem thing in cities and society in the early twentieth century, but was provided massive media attention after 1945. Like the evolving construction of inner city black youth discussed in chapter 2, post-1945 black families were narrated as simple agrarian units struggling in modernist, sprawling cities. This display of "authentic" ghetto family in inner cities showed a raw, roughneck family. Black ghettos were distinctive places, Negroes and their families distinctive people. In these places, black families struggled to socialize youth (see Rainwater 1966; Banfield 1968). These families were said to create a kind of youth, the ghetto kid, who lacked ambition, strong sense of self, and commitment to community and nation.

In the late 1960s and 1970s, work shows, this discourse of problem black families shifted to show more troublesome black families. They were now more "irresponsible" and "lethargic." This offering, taking the form of the tangle of pathology discourse (see Collins 1996; Kennedy 2000), made these families damaging agents in the domain of social reproduction. The abuses ascribed to them were immense: "non-productive," "economically draining," "civically indifferent," in sum destroying America's downtowns by their very presence (see Walter Miller 1958). This enigmatic black family underpinned problems such as depleting tax bases, accelerating downtown erosion, eviscerating central business district vitality, and eroding traditional neighborhood function. Where there was an urban problem, this lurking family had a central connection. In the construction of 1950s and 1960s city issues, it was a fundamental villain.

The post-1980 rendition of black family, already chronicled in content, ultimately communicated persistent understandings by anchoring newness in oldness. Historical "realities" planted in its archive were updated with new wrinkles and facets. The "reality" of a known family met updated content of struggling families to suggest the same truths of group pathology and defective culture. History flourished in this concept as a powerful frame to organize the post-1980 liberal update. Understandings left to thrive undisturbed by superficial update rendered history alive and well in the term. Power lay in activating the term and leaving its foundation undisturbed that summoned up meanings at its core. Use of the term "black family" post-1980, in the final analysis, reaffirmed the power of past discourses dwelling in the concept.

The story of the term "black inner city" is much the same. This term post-1980 similarly unleashed luminous images and meanings: It was widely understood as a damaged social space that created discordant and wild kids. McCarthy (1995), for example, finds in this notion images of families in destructive housing projects, looming kids, bombed-out blocks, dilapidated social and physical fabrics, and teeming masses of ominous people. A 1977 to 1988 survey of popular new journals, moreover, reveals that definitions of "black inner city" moved from a general reference to poverty that included whites, to an exclusive emphasis on the black poor's behavioral and moral characteristics (in Lott 1999). In using this concept, liberals conveyed these images even as they connected it to the likes of economic restructuring, spatial mismatch, and pervasive racism. One more time, liberals failed to confront images and meanings implanted by recent conservative rhetoric.

What was the history stored in this term? Numerous studies reveal this construction's historical roots. In the 1950s, according to Beauregard (1993), black inner cities were made synonymous with slums and underutilized land (see *New York Times* 1953). These spaces were offered as zones of inadequate maintenance that scarred urban downtowns. The supposed dilemma was poor maintenance habits, insufficient commitment to community upgrade, and high rates of unemployment that were creating dilapidation and lowered land values. Plagued by inadequate wages and poor maintenance, this space was purportedly pocked by physical dilapidation and blight. This was Duncan and Beverly's (1957) era of slum crisis, a time when urban slums had supposedly become a national problem.

In the 1960s and 1970s, black inner cities had purportedly evolved into massive ghettos replete with frightful blight, massive rates of unemployment, and serious social isolation from the mainstream (see Merridew 1975a; *Chicago Tribune* 1975). Now they posed an additional danger to cities: they could spread and quickly engulf other areas. Slums, to paraphrase George Romney (in *U.S. News and World Report* 1972a), could spread like wildfire and quickly engulf new areas. The dilemma was their tendency to transmit social ills and cultural pathologies. At the same time, my discussion of this term with people in Chicago, Indianapolis, and St. Louis, asking them to reflect on their inner city in the 1960s and 1970s, yielded similar results. My question provoked images of "troubled ghetto

life," "ghetto uprisings," "urban riots," "inner city violence," "urban renewal," "declining inner city schools," and "deplorable public housing
conditions" (Howard 1987; Beverly 1991).

Post-1980, "black inner cities," like "underclass families," conveyed
understandings with newness stamped into oldness. Foundational truths
stood intact over time while periodic updating continued. The past lived
on in archives as alive-and-well frames of meaning undisturbed by liberal
defining. Past meanings stood firm that provided outline to the essence of
new understandings. The result: liberals spoke of black inner cities affected
by economic restructuring, persistent racism, and job out-migration but
communicated the importance of local culture, inner city space, and
human choice.

History and its past regimes of power were alive and well in these
terms. Failing to purge the past in them, these liberals allowed America's
conservative racialist heritage to live on and to relentlessly push ways to
see and know. This heritage, as detailed in chapter 3, lived on in common
and frequently used terms liberals drew on: black underclass, black inner
city, black politician, black culture, and black youth. As Nietzsche notes,
people should be conscious of being in language. As part of this consciousness, I add, people should recognize language's deep ties to historical regimes of power and domination. Language, to Bakhtin (1981), is
always historically rooted and entangled, possessing an enormous "life-
force" that ensnares and places listeners in worlds of dense meanings. To
believe otherwise is to fall prey to the myth of language neutrality and to
let politics in language persist.

The dilemma these liberals faced, then, was a history stamped in language that transmitted ways to understand. Many now widely acknowledge that history marks the world and creates pathways for seeing by
affecting innumerable things, for example institutional arrangements,
body movements, and established norms in social life. But language also
profoundly bears history, imposing often unacknowledged privileges and
burdens to users in its seemingly natural state. This historical storehouse
captures and retains past histories that sediment like geological layers.
This, I suggest, is one more example of Roland Barthes's (1973) "death of
the author" that rejects the traditional view of author (that is, conserva-

tives and liberals) as discourse originator. To Barthes, texts possess a plurality of meaning that embodies the content of shifting historical power formations.

In practical terms, to Bakhtin (1981), this storage of meanings has different consequences for users. Counter-narrativists are often ineffective because these obscured archives intrude into their communicating. Such narrativists come into conflict with a counter-force that is often superficially understood. Alternatively, status quo narrativists are politically enabled: their dominant meanings spill into oppositional discourses to restrict communication of counter-truths. Prisons of understanding silently forwarded to enable or disable are often only dimly recognized. Offering counter-discourses, I conclude, requires sensitivity to this reality. That is why, to bell hooks (1993), outside of established places of knowledge production, people often struggle to effectively convey their ideas. Concepts betray as people toil to persuade others about their realities. Using borrowed and often betraying concepts, language can be as imprisoning as liberating.

No Determinism

My discussion so far may appear overly deterministic in its seeming straightjacketing of opportunities to transform language and to contest its power. This said, I reject any deterministic position I may seem to be communicating. My position: I believe the power of language and the politics it represents is reversible provided contestation of terminology is penetrating. I submit that this reversal requires two things: (1) creating persuasive alternative truths about issues like "black-on-black violence" that confront dominant versions, and (2) the recognizing of politics of language. With language deeply interrogated, revealed for its politics, and political commitments made elsewhere, dominant language can be undermined. But these liberals, I believe, offered anything but a clear alternative. As carriers of established values, they were only dimly aware of language's power and were too committed to historical meanings in terms previously discussed to seriously contest these meanings.

Examples of successful counter-discourses in the face of meaning-populated language abound. For example, the recent history of gay rights and women's rights movements demonstrates that dominant language is fluid and mutable. These movements have stretched and reconstituted terms in ways that allowed them to effectively speak their truths. They have, paraphrasing Michel Foucault (1971), discovered what terms are and subsequently refused them. Effective use of discourse and sound politics have followed. In these successes, movements have extended politics beyond the realm of action to the realm of language, attacking their empirical references, moral insinuations, and assertions about social reality's supposedly natural state.

The gay rights movement took a national form with two trenchant moments: Anita Bryant's attempt to repeal a Dade County, Florida, gay rights amendment and the Stonewall Riots in New York City. Bryant's highly publicized proposal and rioting because of harassment of gay patrons in a Greenwich Village bar mobilized opposition across the country. Within weeks, politics had "jumped scales" to the national level. Thereafter, the movement attacked the terminology and sense of norms in prevailing sexual-moral discourse. What had started out as "a flash . . . of mass anger" (see *Socialism Today* 1999) quickly led to local and national organizing that problematized the roots of heterosexual-moral discourse. A new organization, the Gay Liberation Front, was formed that spread the message across the country to promote active counter-politics.

Since that time, countless Christian Rights (anti-gay) groups across the country (Oregon Citizens Alliance, Kentucky Families Foundation, Illinois Alliance on Families, Ohio Families Network) have been targets for protest. Contestation has often focused on language and its meanings: what is family, what is marriage, what is equal rights. It is fair to say, without romanticizing or idealizing this movement, that it has recognized language's power and instability. These terms have been seen as extensions of conservative politics and at the root of a constructed homophobia. From the start, the object to attack, according to Stonewall participant Warren Allen Smith (in Kirby 1999), has been obvious: normative heterosexual language. Without power-packed images in words, Smith said, the sense of a natural heterosexual order and moral incriminations against gays would make no sense. Ideological notions like family and marriage, to Smith, have helped construct this naturalness.

In recent years, these terms have been successfully contested in state and local courts. The results have been tangible. In Hawaii, in 1997, after intensive lobbying, a court in Hawaii ruled that denying gays civil rights violated the Hawaii constitution. In 1998, New York City recognized the legal right of gays to equal treatment on everything from housing to parking permits to burial rights. In 1998, a New Jersey Court ruled the Boy Scouts must admit gays, Houston added a gay rights amendment for public employees, Oregon added dual partner benefits for state employees, and the U.S. Supreme Court ruled against same-sex sexual harassment (see Turnout 1998). In this contesting, language has been seen as dialogic, unstable, and a powerful constructor of reality. In the Hawaii case, the terms "civil rights" and "marriage" were attacked before the court (see *National Journal of Sexual Orientation* 1993). In the New York City case, the terms "family" and "equal rights" were made points of controversy (see Teague 1998).

Unlike these liberals who failed to deeply confront terms in the "black-on-black violence" discourse, gay activists did. They reached deeply to connect meanings in terms with visions of reality. A leading crusader in this effort, assassinated San Francisco politician and activist Harvey Milk, noted repeatedly in speeches that the terms "family" and "marriage" formed the basis for creating imagined, normative heterosexual worlds (see Cloud 1998; Turnout 1998). Milk spoke frequently of constructed worlds upon which morality could be preached and normalized. He also spoke of terms that create an imagined normalcy against which deviance can be identified. Milk and others offered the view that naturalized worlds and sense of devious sexuality are inseparable. From this insight, Milk and others successfully contested meanings in terms across the country.

Such political excavation is potentially profound: Terms targeted for their politics can be rendered ineffective. The "politics of the archive" in these terms, in the process, turn counter-productive. So acknowledged, I believe it was possible for these liberals to transform widely held images and meanings in concepts like black inner city, black ghetto, underclass family, and inner city black youth. To persuasively tie black-on-black violence to societal processes in common thought would have required attacking these terms. As in the gay rights movement, counter-narrativists would have had to reveal their rich historical meanings and propose viable alternatives. But liberal renditions of these terms were not like the gay rights movement attack on homophobic concepts: a clear alternative vision necessary to transform these terms was not asserted.

These points are important for counter-narrativists to realize. Terms in current use can be transformed and become defective political property of their most fervent users. Terms at historical moments can move outside a person's or group's ability to use them effectively. Once-potent political forms in this way get robbed of their political content and become politically less useful. With the politics of reality construction obstructed, dominant forces must scramble around and seek other terms to populate with meanings.

Yet let us be clear here: this is no easy task. Even when attacked, terms often prove stubborn. Their images and meanings tend to persist as archives that often elude restructuring. Even as some layers disappear, others often remain intact. Dialogism, alive and well, can revise and modernize but often retains core understandings that sustain tenacious politics. To Wagner-Pacifici (1994), something new can be created but is often made out of something old, new realities deeply borrowing from old realities. Terms used for counter-purposes, paraphrasing Bakhtin (1981), still tend to be at least half someone else's. Such terms become one's own only when narrativists make concerted efforts to populate them with their own intentions and meanings. Without working to overcome this obstacle, terms will serve other people's interests and intentions.

The Outcome

The liberal discourse discussed to this point helped produce a dominant rendition of "black-on-black violence" in mainstream thought. Its discussion of culture, use of spectacle to portray black youth realities, and communication of truths through colonized terms devastated pretensions at being an effective counter-narrative. A youth, made monolithic, was communicated to be deeply bonded to a destructive culture. Black social life in inner cities glistened with seaminess and discordance that seemed different from the life of a normal society. So communicated, the haunt of culture rather than racism, poverty, deindustrialization, or anything else seemed at the center of this urban violence.

This projection of knowledge helped perpetuate something important that needs to be discussed: the recent U.S. history of integrating culture, race, and space to simplify comprehension of people. This integrating of elements has been most active via discourse that chronicles urban blacks. What has been reinforced has been a pervasive stereotype: a black race in inner cities as one more cultural group. This historical creating has led to the likes of T. S. Eliot's proclaiming, "every nation, every race, has not only its own creative, but its own critical turn of mind." With respect to our study of violence, many interviewees in this investigation said similar things. For example, to Indianapolis city councilman Glen Howard (1987), commenting on his city, "race divides the city into communities; that is not surprising. . . . Different cultures live in Indianapolis, that is why we have ethnic enclaves, inner city black neighborhoods, and all kinds of social and cultural communities." Howard was not being intentionally glib or superficial; his honest ideas reflected the seamless meshing of race, space, and culture in common thought.

This race-culture-space integration has formed in common thinking as a "track of thought" to know "inner city blacks." Black skin in this space has become an indicator for beliefs, ways, morals, and conduct endemic to the sense of cultural-spatial group. As in many post-1980 racialized discourses, inner city race has become a stand-in for cultural disposition. I borrow from Etienne Balibar and Immanuel Wallerstein (1996) to suggest that this is America's new racism that is much more consumable than its more traditional variety, biological determinism. This biological form may still lurk deep in thought as co-conspirator, but the construct of culture set in a space has become the new racial indicator. These liberals railed against racism and, I believe, truly opposed racism, but nevertheless reinforced its new form in their rendition of "black-on-black violence." As they strived to humanize inner city black youth in this rendition, they ended up caricaturing them and reinforcing stereotype.

These liberals, black and white, ultimately helped reproduce a cultural racism that conservatives flagrantly and boldly offered. This liberal offering was supported in two ways: it did not pronounce a superiority of whiteness and it did not exclude blackness in the category of legitimate cultural terrain. In the process, it fervently rejected the stereotypes of racism: biologically fixed differences and genetic content as causative for violence. And African Americans that embraced renditions of cultural normalcy were welcomed into the privileged center. But in organizing and explaining social life and violence around a sense of comingling culture, race, and space, inner city African Americans became a stereotyped raced and cultured group that was a social outlier.

In this way, the liberal discourse overtly divested itself of racialist–class privilege. It discussed and rejected the idea of inequitable power relations and racial privilege. But it persisted in comprehending this youth and people through established understandings of culture, race, and space. By repudiating the role of oppressor but reproducing this social template, the sense of problem inner city blacks was sustained. The suggested abhorrence for social and racial hierarchy was ultimately thin: The gaze onto inner cities and society failed to eradicate a prevalent politics of domination.

This cultural racism, like other strands of dominant thought, effortlessly reactivated itself by means of liberals and others thinking along established tracks. It was not the raving of racist subjects or assertions of thinly disguised hatemongers. It rather pivoted around acceptance of deep-rooted beliefs—natural stratification of people into cultural worlds, power of culture to structure human action, race and culture as correspondent realities—that coherently organized thought. These liberals presented themselves as working against flawed conservative thinking, but the absorption of conscious and unconscious beliefs planted this racial-spatial-cultural connection in their thought. At the core of accepting such notions, there were few alternative ways to "see" these things in the mainstream of America.

This communicating by these liberals ultimately devastated their progressive pretensions. The public that was asked to incorporate society into their understanding of "inner city black youth" "saw" culturally bereft and destructive creatures in forbidding terrains. The public was asked to gaze on inner cities with compassion, but for what? As the discourse communicated, these kids were problem beings that willfully tore up lives and neighborhoods in an unapologetic embrace of destruction. Kids hell-bent on undermining or destroying were to be viewed with complex links to society but were fingered as cultural problems. The liberal street manifested bad culture and was the hideous enclave of cultural conversion that kids willingly dived into. In this cultural war zone, society toiled to engage counter-societal kids. That people should allocate compassion for this barbarous lot was an awkward suggestion at best and disingenuous at worst. Asked to feel compassion, many could feel only anger and loathing.

These liberals ultimately occupied an imaginary political left and paid a large price for their discrepancy. Posturing as a conservative counter-voice, they never really communicated a strong alternative. These liberals, too, put themselves in a different place and consciousness from inner city African Americans. Never relinquishing authoritative position that was ostensibly deserved because of their culture, they made themselves culturally normal and outside of black inner cities. To paraphrase bell hooks (1993), they exercised the moral look that continuously disbursed difference and otherness across inner cities. Black inner cities were seen as logical places to scrutinize and judge, where these liberals logically parceled out critique against supposedly troubled and troubling cultural people.

Final Interpretation

Numerous interpretations can be drawn about the failure of these liberal narrativists to substantively differentiate their discourse from that of conservatives. Mine is straightforward: I reject the easy-to-fall-into and reductionist suggestion that they were simply unwitting supporters of foisting America's racial-spatial-cultural sensibilities on this issue. The argument that they were forced to work through the ploy of spectacle and state their case through betraying language is too simple. There were

other stylistic forms to engage the public and a world of possibility beyond hostile communicative constructs to use. The world of stylistic presentation and communicative concepts, rich and varied, extended far
beyond these status quo options. I submit that this liberal complicity was
as much a function of political commitment as political ignorance, that
these liberals were less on the margins of power and unable to effectively
communicate than politically unified with conservative thought.

My point is anything but naïve and simplistic. Indeed, it is rife with
possibilities for constructive politics. On the issue of spectacle, for example, these liberals were capable of rejecting spectacle and its politics in
favor of more dispassionate accounts of struggling sameness and inequitable conditions. Such discussions could have projected the human-
ism these liberals claimed they quested for. Some spectacle, we now know,
opens up "spaces" to caricature and ridicules norms. This liberal staging,
instead, continued a tradition of identifying and criticizing "a people"
who have historically lacked the power to rebuke this tradition in many
urban settings and at the national scale.

The content of prevailing language, at the same time, was ripe for
contestation. These liberals could have confronted foundational beliefs in
terminology. Successful counter-discourses have done this, but these liberals opted to restructure terms in superficial ways. They drew on images
and meanings that intuitively fit their sense of appropriateness and normalcy. This language at the "real" level fit the conceptual commitments of
many liberals. This liberal discourse, then, was ultimately a paradoxical
construct. At one level, it challenged conservative thought but at a more
influential level encoded its power. It offered a more contextually sensitive causative frame for this violence, but in deep beliefs grounded and
reproduced historical-conservative understandings. This liberalism was
anything but a clear, absolute alternative to conservative thought. In
unison with conservativism, liberalism drove a powerful vision of "black-
on-black violence" to dominate mainstream 1980s and 1990s imaginings.

PART THREE

Impacts and Responses

6

The Impacts

The prominent national vision of black-on-black violence emergent in the early 1980s, led by conservative and liberal discussion, had profound impacts on society. In this chapter, I take up one particularly destructive use of this construction: its marshaling in the service of offering a 1980s and 1990s black crime panic across America. I highlight this impact because I believe it was this violence vision's most perverse effect. This dominant vision ("black-on-black violence") and others were mobilized across America to create a villain, black youth, that had far-reaching penal and legislative ramifications. "Black-on-black violence," in this sense, was an issue that came to serve the political purposes of mayors, governors, senators, the penal community, law enforcement, and others as this chapter depicts. This "black-on-black violence" vision, like so many social ills narrated and accepted in the mainstream, became central to the formation of social policy.

The circumstances for this violence vision's being mobilized were straightforward. A slight statistical increase in national crime between 1980 and 1989 (after 1990, crime rates plummeted to record lows; see Stolinsky 2000) in emergent conservative times was a recipe for political advantage. Ronald Reagan realized the possibilities for furthering his law-and-order campaign and conservative agenda by exaggerating this increase. With the "black-on-black violence" discourse and similar constructions, a demonized black youth serendipitously stood available for usage. To exploit this increase in crime, oratory had America under siege by a new horde of criminals—the black predator—taking over cities, suburbs, and rural places. A new criminal was supposedly on the loose and moral crackdown was in order. "He" was the impulsive and roaming

131

being that wreaked havoc on communities. Blaming these kids, something the public could digest, made acceptable a nationwide law-and-order war in general and a crackdown against black youth in particular.

Again, fears and anxieties were collapsed into a trusty urban folk-devil. That it was primitive and racist did not seem to matter. With a sense of a societal crime problem and a need to respond, an already choreo-graphed villain—inner city black youth—was the perfect fill-in. Even when race was not explicitly mentioned, post-1980 pronouncements of the new juvenile predator stalking streets invoked a racial figure everyone knew. This issue, to Mike Davis (1990), was as racially charged as any so-cial issue ever put before the American public. As in previous endeavors to villainize this kid, "he" was to be taken for granted but also to be an ob-ject of unending concern. He, as before, was not to be known by nuanced inspection but by elaborate codification. One more time, urban black kids became pawns in a far-flung political process.

The New Criminal

The resonant images and understandings from "black-on-black violence" fed seamlessly into offerings of who was responsible for the recent upsurge in crime. These images of black youth bestiality were present at the right time for those in charge. "Violent juvenile crime is a national epidemic," declared Representative Bill McCullum (R–FL) in 1985, "and today's su-perpredators are feral, presocial beings with no sense of right and wrong" (in Males 1997). William Bennett, John Walters, and John DiIulio also blamed "the new superpredator" for escalation in crime rates. Their elab-orate images of this ascendant beast in *Bodycount* (1996) were flagrant. As ruthless beings, they said, "[t]he difference between the juvenile criminals of the 1950s and those of the . . . early 1980s was the difference between the Sharks and the Jets of *West Side Story* and the Bloods and the Crips." "It is not inconceivable," to Bennett, Walters, and DiIulio, "that the demo-graphic surge of the next 10 years will bring with it young criminals who make the Bloods and Crips look tame."

This blaming black youth perhaps unsurprisingly soon went beyond "talking-head" oratory to fill standard political forums. The Brookings

Institution, before Congress, explained increased crime by a "new horde from hell that kills, maims, and terrorizes merely to become known, or for no reason at all." Democratic criminologist James Alan Fox, in a widely cited statement, described crime as being driven by a new youth that were "temporary sociopaths, impulsive and immature . . . a 45-year-old with a gun in his hand, though he may be a better shot, is not as likely to use that gun as a 14-year-old." Crime, to Fox, was now dominated by kids that tended to be trigger-happy. "They'll pull that trigger if someone looks at them the wrong way. They'll pull that trigger if someone swears at them. They'll pull the trigger without thinking about the consequences" (in Males 1997). Later Fox, in an AOL forum, noted, "this [juvenile crime] is the lull before the crime storm . . . The future may make [this period] look like the good old days" (see Zoglin 1996).

In this context, conservatives and liberals mobilized "facts" to justify the talk about this youth character. "The new criminal," to the Reagan administration's Justice Department (in Schiraldi 1998), "is male, 15 years and six months old. He has been arrested 11 to 14 times, exclusive of status offenses, and 5 times for felonies. He comes from a dysfunctional family; and in 4.6 percent of the cases, at least one of his parents also has an arrest history." "He," to the Justice Department, "has received long-term and continuing social services from as many as six different community service agencies, including family, youth, mental health, social services, schools, juvenile or police authorities, and continues to drain these resources for years before he is finally incarcerated as a career criminal." This offender was disproportionately young, recidivist, weaned on welfare, black, and dysfunctional.

Susan Estrich (1996), in *USA Today*, writes, "there are 40 million children in the United States today under the age of 10. People wonder whether there is anything that can be done to stop potential superpredators . . . before it's too late." Heather Waldrep, editor-in-chief of the *Southern Nazarene,* notes: "ever heard of a Superpredator? No, it's not a character from Alyssa Milano's latest straight-to-video release. A superpredator is a boy—a teenaged male who defines himself with violent behavior." They offer "mindless, brainless, senseless, emotionless teen-aged violence, all occurring in a relatively small area" (1995, 1). The book

Bodycount similarly notes: "here is what we believe: America is now home to thickening ranks of juvenile superpredators—radically impulsive, brutally remorseless youngsters, including ever more pre-teenage boys, who murder, assault, rape, rob, burglarize, deal deadly drugs, join gun-toting gangs and create serious communal disorders. . . . At core, the problem is that most inner city children grow up surrounded by teenagers and adults who are themselves deviant, delinquent, or criminal" (Bennett, Walters, and DiIulio 1996, 43).

Often, "facts" about youth offenders invoked race. John DiIulio, the most explicit and vocal practitioner of this invocation, notes: "murder, rape, robbery, and assault remain at historic highs . . . [and] not only is the number of young black criminals likely to surge, but also the black crime rate, both black-on-black and black-on-white, is increasing, so that as many as half of these juvenile superpredators could be young black males." DiIulio pronounced himself as practicing "honest discourse" at a time when honesty "about race and crime is shrinking." He adds:

> What are the facts about race and crime? . . . Over the coming decade, juvenile arrests in California and many other states are projected to increase by some 25 percent, even more for minority juveniles. By the year 2005, we will probably have 200,000 convicted juvenile criminals, half of them black males, in secure confinement, including adult prisons and jails—over 3 times more than the number of incarcerated juveniles today. The reason for this will be that more black boys grew up without adults who were willing and able to save them—and their victims. (DiIulio 1996a, 68)

An early practitioner of invoking this crime panic and blaming black youth was Ronald Reagan. Sanitized language barely concealed his anger and loathing for this purported new breed of criminal: "a stark, staring face—a face that belongs to a frightening reality of our time: the face of the human predator . . . Nothing in nature is more cruel or more dangerous" (in Beckett 1997, 47). Reagan's crime problem this way was given a clear, resonant face. It was one the mainstream suspected and distrusted, and one that had been fingered before as responsible for diverse social quandaries (for example, decline of cities, erosion of urban tax bases, white flight from downtowns, decline of public education). Reagan's seizure of the past updated the black youth problem in luminous images. In the past, these kids ominously roamed and devalued much in their wake. Now, these acts translated into out-of-control crime and disorder.

The way to deal with them, to Reagan, was clear: more disciplining and punishing. "Individuals are responsible for their actions; retribution should be swift and sure for those who prey on the innocent" (in Beckett 1997). While invoking caricature as reality, Reagan seamlessly banished society, context, and circumstance in his sketch of these kids. Their reality, to Reagan, was one of unfettered choice, bountiful opportunities, immense possibilities, and unhampered social mobility. In this context, this crime wave was always cast as controllable, reversible, and striking at the heart of society: the average American. In the process, Reagan appeared as a candid spokesperson for the average guy and as an optimist who knew what needed to be done. For example, his remarks at a White House ceremony observing Crime Victims Week received tremendous press and national acclaim: "The crime epidemic threat has spread throughout our country, and it's no uncontrollable disease, much less an irreversible tide. Nor is it some inevitable sociological phenomenon . . . It is, instead, and in large measure, a cumulative result of too much emphasis on the protection of the accused and little concern for our government's responsibility to protect the lives, homes, and rights of our law-abiding citizens" (in Beckett 1997).

In this context, a host of polls was trotted out to justify the need for more punishment of criminals. In a pool of diverse and contradictory polls (see Males 1997), those supporting "get tough on youth" assertion were boldly centered. To the Heritage Foundation (1998), for example, "polls show that Americans are unhappy with the [juvenile justice] system as it is: 49 percent believe rehabilitation programs for juveniles are not successful, 52 percent believe the punishments juveniles receive should be the same as those given adults, and 83 percent think juveniles who commit two or more crimes should receive the same sentencing as adults." Similarly, a 1995 Gallup poll reported by the Heritage Foundation "found that 72 percent of Americans also advocate the death penalty for juveniles who commit murder, as opposed to 64 percent in 1957." And "teenagers themselves take a hard stance on how their peers should be treated if they commit violent crimes. Over 93 percent believe that those accused of murder or rape should be tried as adults. Moreover, they do not believe these offenders should receive special consideration because of their age."

But it is crucial to underscore that the public was profoundly misinformed on this issue. Again, violent crime had steadily dropped and black youth participation in this had waned since 1991. Between 1992 and 1996, homicide in America declined 20 percent but homicide coverage on the ABC, NBC, and CBS evening news increased 721 percent (see Schiraldi 1998). Americans, moreover, thought juveniles committed 43 percent of homicides, yet in reality they committed only 9 percent of these. Nearly two-thirds of Americans thought juvenile crime was on the increase, but this statistic dropped 58 percent in the 1990s (Schiraldi 1998). And to a disproportionate degree, these renditions of juvenile crime featured black urban kids (Males 1999). These bodies continuously flashed across TV screens and pundit essays, reinforcing the notion of the new black predator.

But there was another side to this opportunistic discovery of black youth beasts that needs to be mentioned. In addition to the need to find a simple and digestible scapegoat for rising crime, some could benefit enormously from promoting this connection of black youth and rising crime. Politicians, for example, saw opportunities to advance careers (see Beckett 1997). Thus mayors like Rorty of Los Angeles, Morial of New Orleans, Greene of Philadelphia, and Byrne of Chicago swept into office on this crime panic oratory. Each could invoke this reality, proclaim the need to rigorously police inner cities and enforce laws as deterrents to city decline, and appear tough. To Marc Morial (2000), "mayors are on the front lines of the battle . . . We attend the funerals . . . We comfort the families. We clean up the blood." The same oratory flowed from governors like Wilson of California, Pataki of New York, Jeb Bush of Florida, and George W. Bush of Texas. Each announced their state's cities under siege by the new crime. Paraphrasing Wilson, California's urban centers were experiencing a dangerous escalation of young inner city juvenile criminals and actions had to be undertaken.

Pundits and newspapers across America equally used this issue to their advantage. First and foremost, this was a lens through which they could speak their "truths" about crime, black youth, and society. But in the post-1980 political climate, this strategy also proved rewarding. John DiIulio's incendiary rhetoric warning of a "generational wolfpack" of "fatherless, godless and jobless teens" established him as America's foremost crime guru. Between 1996 and 2000, his coauthored book *Bodycount* sold more than 750,000 copies. The *Washington Post* similarly spoke widely on the new criminals, terming them "the new face of murder" that helped sell newspapers. Its 1995 front-page article that fingered black kids for crime, "The New Face of Murder in America: Family Slayings Decline; Few Cases Solved; Killers Are Younger," sold more copies than any *Post* paper in the decade. Not to be outdone, Bob Dole spoke continuously about crime, which enhanced his ratings. He noted: "unless something is done soon, some of today's newborns will become tomorrow's super predators—merciless criminals capable of committing the most vicious acts for the most trivial of reasons" (in Conquergood 2003, 1).

The Outcome

This social climate that the dominant "black-on-black violence" discourse helped fuel was, not surprisingly, conducive for toughening crime policy. The Reagan administration took the first steps. In 1980 Attorney General William French Smith created the Task Force on Violent Crime to tackle this issue. The goal, paraphrasing Smith, was to eradicate this new youth violence in increasingly violent inner cities and society (see William French Smith 1991). At the same time, the Reagan administration pushed law enforcement agencies to shift attention from white-collar offenses to street crime. Evelle Younger, chairperson of Reagan's Advisory Group on the Administration of Justice, noted: "most of us [the American people] want to focus on violent crime, crime in the streets" (in Beckett 1997). In October 1981, the Justice Department announced its goal to reduce by 50 percent the workers who identify and prosecute white-collar crime. The Justice Department also rejected the "hunt" for other kinds of violence: domestic violence, corporate violence, child abuse. In the words of Younger, it was "not the kind of street violence about which the Task Force was organized."

The first blockbuster crime legislation in the 1980s attacked youth violence in cities: the Comprehensive Crime Control Act of 1984. This policy, with an explicit target, stiffened what was called "too lenient" policy on crime and drugs. Its laws changed bail procedures to allow preventive detainment of "dangerous" offenders, increased prison sentences and fines for distribution or sale of controlled substances, and imposed criminal forfeiture on all felony drug offenses. All three added up to more prison time for offenders, which was heralded as the centerpiece of the new need to attack and clean up the streets. As identified in chapters 3 and 4, drugs and inner city violence were tightly bound issues in common thought. This crackdown on "minority disorder and violence" attacked the purported plagues of easy bail, short sentences, and availability of criminal loopholes to beat convictions.

Congress passed the Anti-Drug Abuse Act less than two years later. Like the previous legislation, drugs and youth violence were the established targets. In the area of extending existing legislation, maximum sentences for drug trafficking were increased, mandatory minimum sentences for drug trafficking and possession imposed, and the scope of criminal and civil forfeiture statues broadened (Scheingold 1991; Beckett 1997). In new legislative provisions, stiff mandatory sentences were imposed on aliens who became drug-addicted or who had prior to U.S. entry been convicted of possessing any amount of cocaine (National Center for Policy Analysis 1997). These "get tough" measures, in policy pronouncement, targeted gangs and drug sellers, the supposed center of the new crime quandary. With a purported scourge of gangs and drugs driving violence, the idea of stiffer sentences, new deportation proceedings, and reduced rights for offenders resonated with Americans (see Schlosser 1998).

Nineteen-eighties crime legislation was the translation of the new moral black panic into policy and law. Among the forces that propelled this action was politicians' realization that they could gain votes by demonizing these kids and demonstrating honest moral toughness. These operatives, paraphrasing Stuart A. Scheingold (1991), knew a good issue when it was staring at them. At the same time, the politics of redistribution ("welfare programs and policies") could be made laughable by "exposing" these kids. The best way to rationalize welfare state retrenchment, in a tack widely used in post-1980s America, is to reveal the grotesque character of its recipients (see Davis 1990; Males 1997). Now ruthless policing and sentencing of black lives became etched into law. Black youth became passive fodder in a broad, national politics. What these kids supposedly were, which could intensify, was a politically strategic invocation for many.

The onslaught of federal legislation on black urban youth continued into the 1990s. In 1991, Joseph Biden successfully introduced two bills in Congress (S.15 and S.618) to spend an additional $4 billion annually to put more police on the streets and to more vigorously enforce existing laws. Three key features dominated. First, $700 million would be spent to build and operate drug prisons. This new system of regional federal prisons, capable of holding twelve thousand total prisoners, accepted from state prisons violent offenders with drug abuse histories. Second, government established an ROTC for police, with $430 million annually to create and finance this Police Corps, which would deepen police training especially in the handling of violent and recidivist youth. At the same time, scholarships would be offered to college students to work in state or local police forces for four years after graduation. Third, government created ten federal military-style boot camp prisons to house first offenders and drug abusers. In each facility, tough discipline would be applied to two thousand to three thousand kids to "rehabilitate them socially."

Clinton's 1993 crime bill was much of the same. It extended the death penalty to fifty-two new offenses (including killing government poultry workers) and funded the hire of 100,000 additional police officers across America (see Hadjor 1997). Democrats and Republicans endorsed the thrust of the legislation. For ultraconservative pundits like John Leo and John Novak, this legislation was good but didn't go far enough; even more police had to be on the streets. The issue, to the Heritage Foundation, was to not let up on the kid "with no moral compass": "[We must] ensure that the guilty go to jail, and once in jail, restrain convicts from jamming the federal courts with frivolous habeas corpus petitions" (see

Heritage Foundation 1994). Now the villain had been unequivocally identified; the American judicial system had to respond accordingly. As these kids rambunctiously walked the streets ("he made up 45 percent of gang members, usually had no father figure in the home, and had siblings with extensive histories of arrest and receiving public assistance"), stern action was needed.

Two years later, federal law strengthened these provisions. The 1995 Violent Criminal Incarceration Act increased funding for state prisons and added incentives for states to curtail early parole. Funds to build state prisons increased 25 percent to $10.3 billion, and grants were provided to states to ensure violent offenders serve at least 85 percent of imposed sentences. Clinton's White House now declared "youth crime its top law-enforcement priority" (see Beckett 1997). These "taking back the streets" provisions were premised on stricter enforcement, stiffer penalties, and more jail time for youth offenders. One more time, kids were located at the heart of a supposed burgeoning crime problem, and cities (read inner cities) were the identified sites for their activities. Clinton was adamant: the judicial system had to be tougher.

In the area of funding new prisons, this 1995 legislation helped support a notorious new entity: supermax prisons across the United States. This legislation stipulated that more prisons and tougher ones were needed to combat rising crime. This initiative was declared top priority by Clinton. Supermax construction was driven, first, by the growing overcrowding of prisons in America. As incarceration rates swelled, most prisons in the United States were operating at well over capacity (National Institute of Corrections 1999). As the National Institute of Corrections puts it, "this crowding aggravated by the increase in street gang members, drug offenders, mentally ill, and youth offenders . . . meant something had to be done." To the National Institute of Corrections, "maintaining order has been a daunting challenge for prison wardens and corrections system administrators." The answer to maintaining order? Build new large prisons to isolate the most serious and chronic "troublemakers."

But construction of the over twenty "supermax prisons" between 1990 and 2000 was also driven by the new sensibility to be tough on offenders. In each case, there was minimal opposition to these flagrantly punitive prisons. John Hurley, the warden at a supermax in Colorado, sees this prison as a shift in emphasis from a "medical model of rehabilitation to a more reality-based approach" (*Village Voice* 1999). Such phrasing, to Mike Males (1997), signals most clearly the new reality of crime prevention: more disciplining and more punishment of prisoners. A 1999 project in Wisconsin illustrates this new kind of incarceration. Its construction in a small rural community locally supported with the promise of employment offers a spartan environment and living conditions (Dorrer 2000). Its main features are complete isolation, small cells, no contact with nature or other people, small slots in steel doors to provide food, and a fixture of electronic doors and fences. In its demographics, original intent has been blurred. First-time offenders are mixed with long-term prisoners, and an estimated 80 percent of the population is black. For those who come into this brutal environment with no psychiatric problems, investigator John Smith notes, such problems will likely be induced (in *Village Voice* 1999).

In the political climate of the 1990s, there was scant public debate about the character of these prisons, that is, their penological justification, their rehabilitative effects of confining people, the high price in terms of misery and suffering it inflicts. As Human Rights Watch (2000) notes, general scrutiny has been limited by the public's tradition of deferring to the judgments of prison officials and by established jurisprudence, both of whom set high thresholds for finding prison conditions unconstitutionally cruel. In this context, to Human Rights Watch, politicians gain popularity by advocating harsh punitive policies for criminal offenders. Elected officials, fearful of being seen as soft on crime, supported supermax prisons for their symbolic message. In sum, neither elected officials, the courts, the public, nor corrections officials opposed proliferation of supermaxes or insisted on improving their conditions.

There was much irony here: by 1998, violent crime in the United States had fallen to a twenty-year low (National Center for Policy Analysis 1998). But there was no stopping production of the crime panic and scapegoating of urban black youth. The results were catastrophic: between 1980 and 1994, the U.S. incarcerated population increased from 500,000 to 1.5 million (+330 percent) (Beckett 1997). In 1997, federal and state prisons housed over one million prisoners, an increase from 250,000 in

1970 (Beckett 1997). In 1990, only nine states operated prisons at or below capacity; the rest were overcrowded by an average of 30 percent. In the process, corrections costs soared: more than $30 billion was spent by local, state, and federal governments on corrections in 1994, an increase from $4 billion in 1975 (see Schiraldi 1998). In California, for example, between 1984 and 1996 the Department of Corrections added 25,864 employees while the higher education workforce was reduced by 8,082 (American Civil Liberties Union 1998). In 1998 California spent more to incarcerate a youth than it did to educate a student ($32,200 per year to house a youth at the California Youth Authority and $5,327 to educate a public student).

The composition of prison populations also changed. In 1992, 51 percent of those incarcerated were black, an increase of 37 percent from twelve years earlier (American Civil Liberties Union 1998). In 1998 almost one in three (32.2 percent) African American men age twenty to twenty-nine were under criminal justice control (in prison, probation, or parole)(American Civil Liberties Union 1998). In Washington, D.C., the figure was 50 percent. In California, where twenty-four new prisons have been constructed since 1984 (twelve prisons were built in the previous 132 years), almost 90 percent of those sentenced to prison for drug possession have been African American or Latino. As Christopher Maxwell and Timothy Bynum (1999) chronicle, the simple visual evidence upon visiting a prison post-1980 was compelling: Most prisoners were young blacks and Hispanics.

In this political setting, an unprecedented number of youths were sentenced to death. Between 1980 and 2000, over four thousand juveniles were sentenced to die (yearly about 2 to 3 percent of all death sentences imposed), with nearly 59 percent of them black (Streib 2000). Almost 70 percent of these sentences have been imposed on eighteen-year-olds, the other 30 percent on kids aged sixteen and seventeen. From 1973 to 2000, 361 juvenile executions were carried out, over half occurring in Texas (Streib 2000). The United States is one of only seven countries that permit executions of youth (American Civil Liberties Union 2000). This practice of killing sixteen-and seventeen-year-olds, upheld in a landmark 1989 U.S. Supreme Court ruling written by Antonin Scalia, continues. Seven states have carried out such executions since 1980: Georgia, Louisiana, Missouri, Oklahoma, South Carolina, Texas, and Virginia. Ironically, this practice continues despite the 1998 UN Commission on Human Rights condemnation of the U.S. death penalty as "arbitrary." Their detailed report states "race, ethnic origin, and economic status appear to be key determinants [in the United States] of who will and who will not receive a sentence of death" (American Civil Liberties Union 2000).

Other Local Responses

But the new juvenile crime panic also extended to local urban and community governance. Post–1980, cities geared up to face this supposed new reality raging across America. The battle now was stepped up, especially with new cutting-edge information technology and surveillance available from the 1983 Serious Habitual Offenders Comprehensive Action Program (SHOCAP). This program gave funds to cities and states to combine community police work, microelectronic communications, and sophisticated data collection. Databases were to be assembled that could track criminals in and across cities. They were to contain personal histories of offenders through information submitted by law enforcement, the courts, probation and parole, juvenile justice, schools, and human services. Touted as the definitive new model to halt juvenile crime by Reagan's Justice Department, it was said to greatly enable pursuit and capture of kids. SHOCAP funds to cities and counties, dependent upon the magnitude of the problem, could be used for no other purpose.

Few cities have used SHOPAC and new programs more effectively than Los Angeles. Fueled by new surveillance data and funds, its "ghettos" became sites for stepped-up raids, sting efforts, and street policing. Central to this effort has been the Gang Related Trafficker Suppression Program (GRTSP) that targeted "drug blocks and neighborhoods" for increased monitoring and raids by two hundred to three hundred police at a time (Davis 1990). GRTSP also sanctioned the routine stopping and interrogating of anyone suspected of being a gang member. From police cars and the street, suspicious-looking kids were profiled and confronted. In the process, over 1,500 arrests ensued in February and March of 1985 alone.

Yet despite questionable tactics, politician support for GRTSP was complete. When queried about the possibility that civil rights of black youth were being violated, Senator Diane Watson's press secretary said, "when you have a state of war, civil rights are suspended for the duration of the conflict" (Davis 1990).

The Los Angeles police department, at the same time, began to institute ad hoc "super sweeps" called the HAMMER in other "ghetto" neighborhoods. These mobile and often brutal sweeps targeted suspected gang members for shakedown, relying upon dress and use of hand signals to identify them. Movement and actions of kids were meticulously recorded and put into the SHOCAP database. Between 1985 and 1990, the combined forces of the LAPD and the sheriffs had picked up close to 50,000 suspects, an incredible figure in view of the fact that there are only 100,000 black youth in Los Angeles (Davis 1990). At the same time, as Mike Davis chronicles, most kids in inner city neighborhoods not surprisingly became prisoners of gang paranoia. Like a plague, fear of the police swept over these areas. Out of fear, many Los Angeles playgrounds, beaches, and entertainment centers became virtual no-go areas for young blacks (Davis 1990).

In Dallas, fear of youth crime led to accelerated surveillance and policing particularly in its poorest area, Gaston. The area, 1.97 square miles with 21,857 residents, has been subject to continuous sting operations, drug busts, and intensive street policing. Between 1983 and 1997, over 35 percent of arrests in Dallas involved people in Gaston, an area comprising less than 6 percent of city population (*Dallas Morning News* 1997). Through intense surveillance, an advanced gang-tracking computer database, and a telemarketing computer system to issue crime alerts, Gaston has been besieged. The leader was the Violent Crime Squad (VCS), extending its tentacles to also become the Violent Crime/Fugitive-Joint Task Force (VC-JTF) in 1992. While the conservative *Dallas Morning News* complained that Gaston had become "a police state" and civil rights were routinely being violated, actions persisted.

In smaller Bloomington, Illinois, the scenario was much the same. Fear of juvenile crime and violence led to massive public investment in science and technology to enhance surveillance and forensic capabilities. In 1983, the police department's Forensic Sciences and Crime Scene Unit added departments in forensic art, bloodstain pattern analysis, crime scene investigation, footwear/tire-track laboratory analysis, polygraph analysis, forensic photography/electric imaging, and voice identification/acoustic analysis (see Bloomington Police Department 2002). The police station, one administrator proudly boasted, looked more like a physics or chemistry laboratory than a police facility (see Hughes 1998). In this context, the city identified eight gangs and 640 gang members for stepped-up scrutiny and policing. Their suspected home, Bloomington's inner city, became the site of intensive surveillance and police sweeps.

Cities across the United States also increasingly turned to curfews after 1980 to combat street crime. San Diego City councilperson S. Golding summed up this strategy of physically regulating youth: "there are nuances in the policy. We're really emphasizing hanging around in public places, because that's where the trouble starts." Curfews typically ban juveniles from public places beyond certain night hours and subject them and parents to potential civic fines (see Males 1997). In 1995, 70 percent of the cities surveyed by the Conference of Mayors had nighttime curfews as part of strategies to halt juvenile crime (U.S. Conference of Mayors 1997). In 1980, in contrast, less than 6 percent of U.S. cities had nighttime curfews. Between 1980 and 1995, 122 cities in the United States adopted curfews (U.S. Conference of Mayors 1997). Yet in many cities, curfews have been challenged. Critics have claimed that they promote a climate of fear, sanction, and random questioning and detention of youths, and that they violate youth's constitutional rights.

To many critics, black youth have been targeted by curfews both legislatively and through monitoring procedures. In Los Angeles, over five thousand young people were arrested for curfew violation in 1986 (see Davidson 1999), many of them in South-Central and other black neighborhoods. Curfew in L.A. became a metaphor for police crackdown in inner city minority neighborhoods (see Males 1997; Males and Macallair 1999). In Chicago, a 1992 anti-loitering-curfew law allowed police to order standing youth to disperse if they believed a kid belonged to a gang.

All youth had to "move along" or be subject to arrest. To supporters, here was an ordinance that helped "clean up the city's worst neighborhoods." Anyone refusing to move could be fined $500, required to perform 120 hours of community service, and spend six months in jail (see Ausick 1997).

Yet all of this effort occurs while much evidence suggests curfews do not deter youth crime. Acts of crime, to Avi Hein of Youthspeak (2000), are not simple nighttime events conducted in public spaces. Crime occurs with or without curfews, according to Hein. Crime, as acts of anger, discord, and hopelessness, resist simple curfew legislation: these are Hein's real human realities that need to be dealt with. The statistics bear this point out. After studying crime rates and curfew arrest data in cities and counties across California, Mike Males and Dan Macallair conclude: "Statistical analysis provides no support for the proposition that stricter curfew requirements reduces youth crime absolutely or relative to adults, by location, by city, or by type of crime. Curfew enforcement generally had no discernable effect on youth crime. In those instances in which a significant effect was found, it was more likely to be positive . . . than negative" (Males and Macallair 1999, 91).

In sum, fear of black youth crime swept over urban America post-1980 that extended to policy and programs. The National Center for Policy Analysis (1997) could have been speaking for all of these aforementioned city administrators when they noted:

> [T]here are 9 facts of crime that everyone had to know: (1) crime is concentrated in urban America; (2) urban crime is increasingly concentrated in inner-city neighborhoods; (3) conditions that foster crime are spreading to poor white communities; (4) more crime involves chronic violent offenders under 18 years old; (5) a small fraction of juvenile criminals commit a majority of all juvenile crimes and become adult career criminals; (6) more cops are needed in inner city neighborhoods; (7) most predatory street criminals spend little time behind bars; and . . . (9) reducing crime requires reducing the number of at-risk juveniles." Inner cities, in the public consciousness, had become gangbang cities, a place of uncontrolled violence that threatened to spread and engulf more civilized spaces.

The post–1980 crackdown on inner cities has had many supporters, most ominously from the genetics-criminality school that gained popularity parallel to America's fear of black youth. This is not meant as guilt by association, but rather to reveal that such explanations are consistent with such policing measures. This post-1980s emergent school has regularly proclaimed support for more punishing crime bills. For example, the leader in post-1980 biological criminology, Sarnoff Mednick, has been especially vocal in this regard. Mednick and his colleagues claim to have discovered what they term the inherited "autonomic nervous system" (ANS) among offenders. Such ANS people are purportedly less sensitive to environmental stimuli. This slow arousal makes them less likely to develop responses necessary to inhibit antisocial behavior. The policy responses from Mednick's proclamation are clear: carriers of noneradicable ANS require segregative containment rather than rehabilitation. Isolation and strict disciplining response, Mednick has said, are the best acts to contain violence (see Hughes 1998).

Mednick agrees with the U.S. National Research Council (which recently sponsored a fifteen-year study to examine the effects of 100,000 genes on criminal activity) that this biological connection needs more study (see Hughes 1998). At the same time, Mednick believes that the key to mitigating crime is more discipline. Recently he compared criminal histories of thousands of young criminals in Copenhagen and Philadelphia and noted consistent punishment was the key (see Reynolds 1998). Punishment delivered after every offense, to Mednick, substantially reduced later offenses. Alternatively, offenders earlier punished for crime but who received nothing for later offenses resumed criminal activity at higher rates. "The way to reduce prison populations," Mednick writes, "is to punish offenders from their first offense with graduated, increasingly severe, and certain sanctions." "The big problem with our handling of criminals in America," to Mednick, "is that they're not punished."

Reflecting Back

As we reflect back on this 1980s and 1990s rise of punitive legislation and policy, it must be added that many saw the 1990s as a period in which the

Reagan-era and Bush-era responses might be halted. In particular, some believed Bill Clinton's election in 1990 would alter the course of get-tough youth politics. His record was vague on what could follow and no one knew for sure. On the one hand, Clinton spoke widely on the need for more vigorous law enforcement and on the goal to establish boot camps for youth offenders, and touted a record of capital punishment (see Clinton Press Release 1994). He presented himself as a law-and-order guy who would carry this law enforcement to its logical conclusion. On the other hand, Clinton provided clues for the need to change current legislative and policing strategies. Speeches sporadically identified the complex social conditions—poverty, inequality, structural unemployment—that tended to beset the actions of criminals (see Clinton 1995). Clinton here spoke about government's responsibility to tackle the reality of prevailing inequalities, notably in the area of acquiring jobs.

But significant change in policy never materialized. To Beckett, Clinton's 1993 anti-crime package was a near clone of the Republicans'. Clinton called for more police, for enhanced federal support for prison construction, and for limits on habeas corpus appeals. The Republican package announced one week earlier in 1993 was a near duplicate. The only difference between the two approaches was the issue of gun control. With the results of elections that year seen as expressions of the public's desire to be tough with youth criminals, the die was cast. Yet, to Beckett, the publicity from this legislation appears to have affected public opinion; those polled who felt crime was the country's most important problem increased from 9 percent to 22 percent to 32 percent from June to October to January of 1994. Clinton reinforced this thrust in his 1994 State of the Union address, urging Congress to adopt the federal equivalent of California's three-strikes law.

From then on, Democrats supported tougher sentencing laws, greater policing, and more prison construction. Many Democrats were pleased that poll results across the decade showed Republicans no longer enjoying an advantage on the crime issue. Sporadic criticism from some Democrats did not deter them from trying to seize the law-and-order issue. In crime bills passed by the House in February 1995, federal grants for state prison construction increased $12.6 billion, the scope of court-ordered settlements in prison-condition lawsuits was restricted, and provisions for swift deportation of illegal immigrants strengthened. Clinton's failure to provide a meaningful alternative to Republicans was explained away by one administration official: "[You] can't appear soft on crime when crime hysteria is sweeping the country. Maybe [someday] the national temper will change . . ." (in Beckett 1997, 61).

I would be remiss not to mention the impact of George H. W. Bush's 1988 notorious invoking of Willie Horton on TV on democratic thought. This ad as much as anything helped shape the democratic sense of appropriate response to the crime issue. This invoking, which destroyed Michael Dukakis's presidential bid, mobilized perceptions that Democrats like Dukakis could not be soft on crime, especially black criminals. This display of a degenerate black man who brutally raped but eluded incarceration resonated with the public. As Mike Davis (1990) explains, this act terrified liberals and reinforced the idea that they had to appear ruthless with juvenile youth. And even left-of-Democrat people were silenced by the power of this image. An interview with ACLU leader Joan Howarth sums this situation up: "progressives have virtually deserted us on this issue . . . the Left has been largely shut out of the policy debate which is now totally framed by the Reaganite Right and its democratic shadow. There is no progressive agenda on crime, and consequently, no challenging of the socio-economic forces that have produced . . . burgeoning . . . gang membership" (in Davis 1990, 123).

In the end, Democrats and Republicans unified around the "get tough on youth" theme. Democrats, whether feeling these convictions or deciding to take the pragmatic road, were central to advancing this agenda. In the process, black youth became used by the mainstream political apparatus. Virulent programs and policies targeting them for aggressive surveillance and management promised to restore law and order. Punitive camps and prisons that soon disproportionately housed African Americans promised to cleanse cities and society. That this youth-punishing drive rested on fuzzy and very disturbing assumptions about these kids did not seem to faze many democrats. Appeal to hoary prejudices of race and class, in the final analysis, became subsumed under political expediency.

Legacy of the Crackdown

There is, not surprisingly, more than a touch of sad humor in the post-1980 crackdown on urban black kids that the dominant "black-on-black violence" discourse helped fuel. Searching for new tough tactics and sizzle sound bites, politicians postured to demonstrate how tough they could be. In March 1994, for example, congresswoman Deborah Pryce (R-OH) played to images of swelled black predators and attached an amendment to the Omnibus Crime Bill to ban weightlifting equipment in federal prisons. Pryce said "we are supplying a means for many prisoners to significantly increase their strength and bulk, making future acts of violence more likely" (see Taylor 1996). One year later, representative Steve Chabot (R-OH) successfully included the amendment in the Violent Incarceration Act of 1995. "Too many criminals spend their time in prisons becoming even more violent criminal machines," Chabot said. "We need more books in prison and less weight-lifting equipment." Chabot said this, ironically enough, just after law barred prisoners from receiving Pell Education Grants (see Taylor 1996).

This move has been one part of the larger no-frills legislative initiative to make prison life more punishing. Efforts to eliminate inmate privileges have been introduced from diverse sources: state legislatures, governors, commissions of corrections, and sheriffs (Finn 1996). Thus, in 1995, the Mississippi legislature mandated use of striped uniforms with the word *convict* etched on the back, banned televisions and other electronic equipment in cells, and eliminated weight-lifting equipment for inmates. A "No-Frills Prison Act" introduced into Congress in 1995 and enacted in 1996 prohibited TVs, coffee pots, and hot plates in federal cells. In 1994, the Arizona Department of Corrections instituted a chain gang in each of the state's three prisons. Inmates did not have telephone or visitation privileges and recreation was limited to basketball on weekends (Finn 1996). In recent interviews with corrections experts and prison managers, most agreed the stimulus behind these statutes has been legislators seeking to demonstrate their toughness on crime (Finn 1996).

The United States now wears the post-1980 get-tough-on-black-kids trend awkwardly. Over the past twenty years, California has built twenty-one new prisons, added thousands of cells to existing facilities, and increased its inmate population eightfold (Schlosser 1998). Black nonviolent offenders make up the bulk of new additions (Schlosser 1998). Today, the number of imprisoned drug offenders is more than twice the number of inmates for all crimes in 1978. California has the biggest prison system in the Western industrialized world, 40 percent bigger than that of the Federal Bureau of Prisons. In liberal Wisconsin, the state prison system doubled between 1998 and 2002, from 10,551 to 20,255 people (Wilayto 2000). These figures, moreover, came out before the advent of Truth in Sentencing laws and do not include the thousands of prisoners in local jails. In Wisconsin, African Americans make up 5 percent of the state population but 48 percent of state prisoners (Wilayto 2000).

As young blacks are locked up in record numbers, prisons across America are hopelessly overcrowded (Pamela Oliver 2000). The United States now imprisons more people than any other country; Eric Schlosser (1998) believes this number to be a half-million more than in Communist China. Since 1980 approximately one thousand new prisons have been built in the United States. In the process, these prisons have been heavily filled by African Americans. In 1997, for example, 3.2 percent of all black males in the United States were in prison, a percentage 6.6 times higher than the 0.5 percent rate for non-Hispanic white males (Pamela Oliver 2000). Since 1997, this figure has stayed constant. To date, the trend of new policing—intensive (high-tech) police sweeps, stiff sentences, and harsh prisons—targets and disproportionately incarcerates urban black youth.

The post-1980 "black-on-black violence" discourse was not the only issue that fueled this black crime panic and legislative crackdown, but it profoundly contributed. This discourse, driven by conservatives and liberals, castigated black youth and communities that underscored the people who could easily stand in as explanation for a purported escalation of crime nationally. To know these kids through the "black-on-black violence" discourse was to feel fright, anger, repugnance, and the desire to further incriminate them. The discourse, in this sense, helped establish the being that could easily be plugged into construction of a new national crime epidemic. This production of a national crime epidemic had its own political dynamic; the "black-on-black violence" discourse seamlessly fed into it.

7

Contesting the Vision

Cultural Racism and Black-on-Black Violence

This book has documented the rise of a dominant "black-on-black violence" vision that has advanced a kind of cultural racism. This violence vision defies easy attempts to pinpoint its racist roots. Negro-ape mythology no longer flourishes in it; instead a common understanding of race works through notions of culture and space. Common thought has largely rejected biological determinism but widely substitutes spatial-cultural disposition. Urban African Americans become understood as place-based beings carrying so many cultural attributes that capture an irrefutable essence. In this context, racial stereotype continues to flourish in a dimly recognized and taken-for-granted process of representing. The dilemma is that even allegedly sensitive, sympathetic depictions of crime and inner city life are tainted by this template of "seeing." Applied by conservatives and liberals, this new racism conceals its existence under the auspices of sensitivity and concern.

This kind of racism, not surprisingly, creates a dilemma: taken-for-granted prejudice can coexist with the most tolerant support for racial diversity. With social and racial authority superficially obliterated, their unspoken power can be concealed and persistent. Like before, seeing primitivism by reading skin color is sustained in everyday life. This racism is not a blunt hatred and bigotry, but a frequently benevolent, colonizing gaze that finds inner cities inhabited by black beings in natural states. In inner city America, in the fantasy, one finds the implanting of little atavistic African villages. These villages, like their African counterparts, contain people whose ways perpetuate the natural essence of "a people."

153

Stereotype, simplicity, and politics mark this representing of urban black youth and community. Astonishingly, this stereotype is pronounced even at the level of identifying inner city blacks as a demographic group (the starting point of the vision). A racial monolith is presented that fails to capture a diversifying and expanding demographic slice. Let me explain.

Post-1980, the term "inner city black" was increasingly obsolete in a fundamental way: blackness had become diverse and heterogeneous. From New York to Los Angeles to Cleveland to St. Louis, blackness was accommodating a plethora of new ethnicities (that is, people with diverse points of origin, ways, beliefs, and practices). Here blackness increasingly embraced an expansive spectrum of nationalities, languages, and ethnicities, accommodating, for example, Caribbean immigrants like Jamaicans, Trinidadians, and Haitians. The influx of Hispanic blackness from Panama, the Dominican Republic, and Costa Rica was also active and ongoing (see Laws 1997). America's inner cities became places of residence for a potpourri of people that burst the bounds of simple racial categorizations. Thus Harlem, the spiritual capital of Black United States, was more than 25 percent Spanish-speaking in 1980 (U.S. Census Bureau 1980a). In 1990, it was more than 40 percent Spanish-speaking (Marable 1995). The most infamous African American community in Los Angeles, South-Central, was 17 and 37 percent Spanish-speaking in 1970 and 1980 (U.S. Census Bureau 1970 and 1980a).

But to recognize this diversity was to destroy the ground upon which caricature of black youth and black communities could proceed. America in the late 1970s was struggling: the popular consciousness in many settings was not stimulated to absorb and reflect on the changing nature of a convenient demon. In the early 1980s, U.S. cities continued to decline and attempts at symbolic and material recapture had intensified. These structural realities, guiding the media and common thought to find simple causes for urban problems, again found the already stigmatized black kid and black community convenient villains. Issues like "black-on-black violence," then, were efficiently and plausibly made. This villain, made through this and other paralleling discourses post-1980, was expedient and political.

The U.S. capitalist experience was thus at the heart of producing these understandings about black-on-black violence. The ebb and flow of economic-political turbulence and city change were critical. The popular conscience and material might of America rode crests of triumph and navigated falls in the flow of empire. Dominance and imperialist sensibilities nurtured by a powerful economic-political engine had generated unprecedented wealth and global dominance. But its economic and symbolic engine, cities, increasingly fell into crisis in the postwar years. And with crises of accumulation and international political eclipse in the mid and late 1970s, stepped-up attempts at renewal were aggressively sought. These attempts took the fundamental form of seeking to reestablish the material and symbolic basis of cities, all of which pointed to finding easy internal villains that purportedly stood in the way of progress.

Space and Social Understanding

Space, we now know, helped construct the dominant rendition of this urban violence. It was a key resource in building this understanding. But, as discussed in a moment of reflection, this use of space was anything but surprising. Society (and narrativists) after 1980 had become increasingly sensitive to space in their everyday lives. For example, globalization exploded across common thought in the late 1970s as explicitly spatial process. The public was provided images of wheeler-dealers hooked on speedy transactions across countries and continents, an international financial system governed from faraway places, and new telecommunications technologies that glided smoothly over regional spaces. These themes were demonstrably treated in expositions on globalization from *Harvard Business Review* (1977) and *U.S. News and World Report* (1986). Newspapers from *New York Times* to *Los Angeles Times* regularly wrote editorials on globalization and the international economy through the 1980s and 1990s. The imagining of a world under the sway of a new form of business, finance, and technology took hold. To know globalization, in other words, was to be sensitized to space as a thing in reality.

Similarly, post-1980 America again dramatically engaged the discourse of immigration-invasion that made space central. Presidents Ronald Reagan, George W. Bush, and Bill Clinton, in slightly different ways, made immigrants from Mexico, Latin America, the Caribbean, and Southeast Asia domestic concerns and problems to national beliefs and practices (see Diamond 1995). Congress tirelessly invoked issues of immigrant cultural difference, problems in assimilation, and likelihood of legal problems in extradition (see Dorothea Schneider 1988). America was openly provided images of invasion, spatial penetration, and transgression. Space in this was the frame that provided the discourse meaning. This frame, of course, had been offered in the context of immigration fears many times before, but as Harold Bauder (2001) observes, never as explicitly and profoundly as in the post-1980 period. To make sense of this discourse was to center space as something potentially violated and in need of protecting. This discourse, like the previous one, asked the public to think about and reflect upon space.

Waging the Struggle

A point of optimism: I agree with Manning Marable (1995) that "racing" of urban violence is not inevitable and unchangeable. Pockets of local thought (cities, counties, communities) are most easily changed, and such movements could conceivably "jump scales" and become regional or national undertakings. But the starting point in any place must be to tackle the most common categories that people apply to this place: black inner city, black youth, black politicians, black culture, and black families. These historically resonant terms need their politics to be revealed. Their foundations, intricately bound up with power and politics, must be exposed as meaning-laden building blocks for discourses that help distribute societal privileges and resources. So revealed, the public can begin to eye the damage and destruction wrought from such concepts. Marable (1995) calls this undertaking "representational transformationalism," a political movement rooted in a battle over the politics of language, symbols, and vision.

What must be revealed, for example, is that the concept "inner city culture" grounds this prominent "black-on-black violence" vision. It is as widely invoked in the discourse as the notion of black-on-black violence itself. This notion, in use, transmits a constellation of meanings and images: dark and aberrant social spaces, zones of youth dysfunction, places of eccentric families, a non-normative and destructive terrain. This history of meanings sedimented into a term reflects its past usage, a usage that sticks to it. This building block in the discourse seeds and spreads meaning to other terms and to this violence process itself. It, in the process, shoots out understandings about "a people" and "a place" that stage the ground to understand a process ("black-on-black violence").

But what sustains this term and its images complicates the task. It, like other prominently used terms in the discourse, has been elaborately reproduced as a commonly referenced category to quickly and efficiently know the world. Writers, reporters, commentators, and academics have been crucial actors. Their reportage, commentaries, and studies of cities and urban problems have been fundamental mechanisms of reproduction. But in the flow of everyday life, people too have been equally instrumental in reproducing this term. Conversations in informal settings have been as crucial to sustaining this term's life and meanings as anything. In the everyday, this concept has allowed "a people" and "a youth" to be easily identified, mapped and situated in an easy cause-effect formula. The problem is sustained: embedded in a casual concept are potent meanings that caricature and afflict.

But revealing the politics of such categories should be a first step in a broader transformation: to demystify the supposed neutrality of understanding this violence as "black-on-black violence." At stake is cultivating a core understanding: how people unconsciously re-create and legitimate ideologies of race and inequality every time they absorb this rendition of urban violence. People who understand this violence as "black-on-black violence" reproduce an organized system of privilege and rebuke that draws strength from cultural-racial understandings. To accept and absorb this system is to replicate a history of devastating racial understandings. Politics, it must be shown, is everywhere in this understanding—in how African Americans and their communities are seen and in how the "outside" world is presented. To politicize this construction this way is to begin to overhaul it and to set the stage to supplant other similar racial understandings.

Yet this organizing against the language and image in "black-on-black violence" is easier said than done. Who is to take the lead? How are such leaders to be made more aware of the politics of language and the image as they are manifest in the notion "black-on-black violence?" And how can such strategies be successful? I believe that the leaders must be organizers in inner city America, whose constituencies suffer most from this constructing. Heads of community groups, block associations, tenant groups, politicians, and religious leaders see the pain and humiliation in residents carrying the stigma of supposedly bad culture and socially off-the-map youth. These are the people that need to talk to the media, writers, residents, and others about their use of language and communication of politics. No one is as strategically positioned to talk to about this subject effectively.

But how are such leaders to be made aware of the politics of this language and vision? The answer is simple. A growing number of inner city organizers have come to identify problems with this language and vision, but more need to be aware. Across urban America today, numerous groups strike out against racist stereotypes of African Americans and the languages and images in "black-on-black violence" that further these stereotypes. Such leaders are often attuned to the power of language and image by a rich history of activism and social engagement. In Philadelphia, Indianapolis, and Chester, Pennsylvania, for example, advocacy coalitions spearheaded by local churches draw attention to persistent rates of crime inflicted on blacks and crime's correlates of catastrophic job loss, poverty, and hopelessness. They forcefully attack language and meanings in "black-on-black violence" visions and how these help construct a dominant perception of out-of-control, culturally dysfunctional kids wreaking havoc on community. A politics of blaming youth, to leader Kirk B. Jones, is rooted in producing images and meanings of community and population. In targeting language, these groups fight to highlight the debilitating racialized content in terms like "underclass culture," "gang-bangers," "the streets," "ghetto families," "welfare mothers." Today, similar groups in Detroit, Cleveland, Buffalo, and Baltimore have emerged.

These are the people that must continue to fight and to communicate their success stories to leaders in other settings. Like every successful national civil rights struggle (for example, over housing, busing, urban renewal), communication between activists must be ongoing, constructive, and detailed. What was successfully problematized (for example, the political content in terms and images, how these were successfully centered as problems) and what was proposed as alternative must be communicated. Leaders, then, have to be willing to share their experiences openly and constructively. Any impulse to protect successful political strategies must be overcome for the good of building a broader political movement.

And once this political movement gains ascendancy and comes up against masses of people, I believe it can grow. The key to the power of the "black-on-black violence" discourse is its taken-for-grantedness. Its use in the everyday, perpetuating a dimly understood form of racism, influences as a frequently unacknowledged set of meanings pervasively flowing through "circuits of understanding." Many people, I believe, would balk at its use if they realized its racist underpinnings. Some would persist; many others would find their sanctioning of racism objectionable. In this context, the need is to cultivate a central understanding: this language and its images castigate and humiliate children, kids, and families in black America in their purveying of meanings. People who understand this violence as black-on-black violence sustain a racialized hierarchy in America that damages millions of people.

The struggle to supplant the meaning system of "black-on-black violence" is ultimately a contest over identities of black youth and the sense of their communities. As long as this violence is discursively framed as a spectacle of wilding kids in wild and wooly black neighborhoods, it will continue to resonate as "black-on-black violence" and perpetuate racism. But the discourse doesn't have to be this way. Confronting the image-laden character of this construction can restructure thought about it. The key is the formula I have described. Instead of the dominant icon being agency-infused kids rambunctiously roaming inner cities, it could be hurt, hopeless, and searching youth in societally created settings. The reality of rampant underemployment, opportunities confined to dead-end service occupations, evaporation of public resources, and stigmatizing rhetoric can replace the "truth" of freewheeling kids in opportunity-laden but culturally dysfunctional settings. The job has begun; the task now is to build upon it.

References

*, *, *

Index

References

Abrahams, R. D. 1964. *Deep Down on the Jungle.* Hatberg, Miss.: Folklore Associates.

Adelman, Murray. 1988. *Constructing the Political Spectacle.* Chicago: Univ. of Chicago Press.

Alexander, Elizabeth. 1996. "We're Gonna Deconstruct Your Life." In *Representing Black Men,* edited by Marcellus Blount and George P. Cunningham, 131–56. New York: Routledge.

American Civil Liberties Union. 1998. "Criminal Justice in Black and White." *ACLU News,* July/Aug., 1–3.

———. 2000. "Ranks of Youth on Death Row Growing." Aug., technical report, available from author.

American Prospect. 1998. "The Rise and Fall of Racialized Liberalism." *American Prospect* 40 (Sept.): 1.

Anderson, Elijah. 1993. *Streetwise.* Chicago: Univ. of Chicago Press.

Angone, Robert. 1981. "Fighting Gang Crime, Chicago's Rite of Spring." *Chicago Sun-Times,* Mar. 25, 56.

Aubry, Larry. 1987. "The Invisible Wall." *Los Angeles Sentinel,* Mar. 19, A-12.

Auletta, Ken. 1975. "After the Storm, the Hurricane." *Village Voice* 20 (Sept. 1): 8.

Ausick, Diana. 1997. "Curfews: The Bad, the Ugly and Some Good News Too." Research report, Center on Juvenile and Criminal Justice, San Francisco, California.

Bakhtin, Mikhail. 1981. *The Dialogic Imagination.* Austin: Univ. of Texas Press.

Balibar, Etienne, and Immanuel Wallerstein. 1996. *Race, Nation, Class: Ambiguous Identity.* London: Verso.

Banfield, Edward. 1968. *The Unheavenly City.* Boston: Little, Brown and Co.

Barthes, Roland. 1972. *Myth Today.* New York: Hill and Wang.

Bauder, Harold. 2001. "Agency, Place Scale: Representations of Inner-City Youth Identities." *Tijdschrift Voor Economishe en Sociale Geografie* 92: 279–90.

Beauregard, R. A. 1993. *Voices of Decline.* Oxford, UK: Blackwell.

Beckett, Kathryn. 1997. *Making Crime Pay.* New York: Oxford Univ. Press.

Bennett, William, John Walters, and John DiIulio. 1996. *Bodycount: Moral Poverty and How to Win America's War Against Crime and Drugs.* New York: Simon and Schuster.

Berger, L., and W. Luchmann. 1966. *The Social Construction of Reality.* Chicago: Univ. of Chicago Press.

Bernstein, Richard. 1988. "Twenty Years after the Kerner Report: Three Societies, All Separate." *New York Times,* Feb. 29, B-8.

Beverly, Devira. 1991. Near West Side community leader, City of Chicago. Interview by author, June 8.

Blount, Marcellos, and George P. Cunningham. 1996. *Representing Black Men.* London: Routledge.

Boghassian, P. 2001. "What Is Social Construction?" *Times Literary Supplement,* Feb. 23, 14–21.

Bourne, Larry. 1993. "The Demise of Gentrification? A Commentary and Prospective View." *Urban Geography* 14:95–107.

————. 1996. "The Myth of Gentrification." *Urban Studies* 12:408–34.

Boyer, Christine M. 1983. *Dreaming the Rational City.* Cambridge, Mass.: MIT Press.

Bragg, Rick. 1994. "Children Strike Fear into Grown-Up Hearts." *New York Times,* Dec. 2, A-2.

Bromley, Ray. 1997. "Globalization and the Inner Periphery: A Mid-Bronx View." *Annals of the American Academy of Political and Social Science* 551 (May): 191–207.

Browsher, Prentice. 1980. *People Who Care: Making Housing Work for the Poor.* Washington, D.C.: Jubilee Housing.

Brunner, Diane DuBose. 1999. *Between the Masks: Resisting the Politics of Essentialism.* Lanham, Md.: Rowman and Littlefield.

Buck, Nick, and Norman Fainstein. 1992. "A Comparative History, 1880–1973." In *Divided Cities: New York and London in the Contemporary World,* edited by Susan S. Fainstein, Ian Gordon, and Michael Harloe, 29–67. Oxford, UK: Blackwell.

Buer, Dennis L. and John Dzieken. 1987. "Picking Up the Pieces." *Chicago Tribune,* Oct. 18, magazine section.

Burawoy, Michael. 1979. *Manufacturing Consent: Changes in the Labor Process under Monopoly Capitalism.* Chicago: Univ. of Chicago Press.

Burke, Kenneth. 1969. *A Grammar of Motives.* Berkeley: Univ. of California Press.

Burnier, DeLysa, and David Descuter. 1992. "The City as Marketplace: A Rhetorical Analysis of the Urban Enterprise Zone Policy." In *Reagan and Public Discourse in America,* edited by Michael Weiler and W. Barnett Pearce, 251–65. Tuscaloosa: Univ. of Alabama Press.

Business Week. 1979. "Smaller Cities, with No End to Suburbanization." *Business Week,* Sept. 3, 204–9.

Call, B. 1987. Head, Department of Metropolitan Development, City of Indianapolis. Discussion with author, July 19.

Casey, Jim, and Hugh Hough. 1981. "Cabrini-Green Carnage: Nine Die in Two Months." *Chicago Sun-Times,* Mar. 11, sec. 3, 1.

Center for Reclaiming America. 1997. "Inner City Renewal: Issues Tearing Our Nation's Fabric." Technical report, available from center, Fort Lauderdale, Florida.

Chandler, Artura. 1986. Head, Forest Manor Multi- Service Center, Indianapolis. Discussion with author, May 24.

Cheyfitz, Eric. 1981. *The Poetics of Imperialism.* New York: Oxford Univ. Press.

Chicago Defender. 1988a. "Black Institutions and Groups Need Help." *Chicago Defender,* Jan. 11, 9.

———. 1988b. "Needed: Black Agenda for the '90s." *Chicago Defender,* Tuesday, Jan. 5.

Chicago Sun-Times. 1981a. "A City of Contradiction." *Chicago Sun-Times,* May 3, 18.

———. 1981b. "U.S. Violent Crime Rises 13 Percent: Chicago Third Worst." *Chicago Sun-Times,* Apr. 1, 34.

Chicago Tribune. 1978. "Crime, Unemployment Blacks' Top Problems." *Chicago Tribune,* Oct. 16, 1.

———. 1984. "The Real Victims of Gangs." *Chicago Tribune,* Dec. 31, 20.

———. 1994. "Neighbors Take Back the Streets." *Chicago Tribune,* Sept. 18, 4.

City of Bloomington. 2002. www.cityhall.ci.bloomington.il.us/.

Cleaver, Jim. 1987. "The Tragedy of Our Youth." *Los Angeles Sentinel,* Nov. 4, A-7.

Cleveland Call & Post. 1992. "Mayor's Task Force to Hold Hearings on Black-on-Black Crime." *Cleveland Call & Post,* Apr. 16, 4.

———. 1994. "It's not the Message, It's the Messenger." *Cleveland Call & Post,* Mar. 3, 3.

Clinton Press Release. 1994. "President Clinton Announces New Crime Bill Grants to Put Police Officers on the Beat." Oct. 12, www.stungunresources .com/1994_bill_crime_federal.html.

Clinton, William. 1995. "Transcript of President Clinton's Speech on Race Relations." Speech at Univ. of Texas, Oct. 17, Clinton Presidential Archives, Clinton Presidential Center, Little Rock, Arkansas.

Cloud, John. 1998. "Harvey Milk." *Time 100 Polls.* www.time.com/time/ time100/heroes/profile/milk01.html.

Cochran, Thomas. 2001. "The U.S. Conference of Mayors and Business Leaders—A New Political Force." Mayors Business Council, U.S. Conference of Mayors, Washington, D.C..

Collins, Sheila. 1996. *Let Them Eat Ketchup.* New York: Monthly Review.

Conquergood, Dwight. 2003. "The Power of Symbols." Gang Resources Home page, www.gangresearch.net/gangresearch/Media/Power.html.

Cresswell, Tim. 1996. *In Space, Out of Space.* Minneapolis: Univ. of Minnesota Press.

Davidson, Jean, and William Ricktenwald. 1984. "City Leaders Unite to Fight Gang Violence." *Chicago Tribune,* Nov. 27, 1.

Davidson, Margaret. 1999. "Do You Know Where Your Children Are?" essay, www.reason.com/9911/fe.md.do.html.

Davis, Mike. 1990. *City of Quartz.* London: Verso.

Dear, Michael J. 1976. "Abandoned Housing." In *Urban Policy-making and Metropolitan Dynamics: A Comparative Geographical Analysis,* edited by J. S. Adams. Cambridge, UK: Ballinger.

De Certeau, Michel. 1984. *The Practice of Everyday Life.* Berkeley: Univ. of Calif. Press.

Dector, Midge. 1992. "How the Rioters Won." *Commentary,* December, 17–22.

Delgado, Richard, and Jean Stefancic. 2001. *Critical Race Theory: An Introduction.* New York: New York Univ.

Denby, Paul. 1986. "Terror." *Los Angeles Sentinel,* May 15, A-6.

DeParle, Jason. 1996. "Slamming the Door." *New York Times Magazine,* Oct. 20, 14–21.

Diamond, Sarah. 1995. *Roads to Domination: Right Wing Movements and Political Power in the United States.* New York: Guilford.

DiIulio, John. 1996a. "My Black Crime Problem, and Ours." *City Journal* 6 (Spring): 2.

Dorrer, Hildegard. 2000. "The Supermax." Paper presented at Prison Awareness Week, Univ. of Wisconsin, Oct. 22–28, Madison, Wisconsin.

Duany, Andres, 2001. "Three Cheers for Gentrification." *American Enterprise Online,* Apr./May.

Duncan, Otis, and D. Beverly. 1957. *The Negro Population of Chicago: A Study of Residential Succession.* Chicago: Univ. of Chicago Press.

Ehrenhaus, Peter. 1993. "Culture Narratives and the Therapeutic Motif: The Political Containment of Vietnam Veterans." In *Narrative and Social Control,* edited by D. Mumby, 53–81. Newbury Park, Calif.: Sage.

Epstein, Jason. 1976. "The Last Days of New York." *New York Review of Books* 23 (Feb. 19): 22.

Estrich, Susan. 1996. "Violent Kids Can't Be Reformed." *USA Today,* Feb. 6.

Europe Traveled. 1991. "Northern Ireland and Ireland: Violence and Literature." Available from author.

Fair, Jo Ellen, and Roberta J. Astroff. 1991. "Constructing Race and Violence: U.S. News Coverage and the Signifying Practices of Apartheid." *Journal of Communication* 41 (Autumn): 58–73.

Fairclough, Norman. 1992. *Discourse and Social Change.* New York: Polity.

Fang, Eric C. Y. 1998. "Urban Renewal Revisited: A Design Critique." Available from author.

Fernandez, Elizabeth, and Phillip Matier. 1988. "Teen-Age Violence Haunts the City." *San Francisco Chronicle,* Feb. 21, sec. 3, 1.

Finn, Peter. 1996. "No Frills Prisons and Jails: A Movement in Flux." *Federal Probation* 60, no. 3, 35–44.

Fitzpatrick, Dan. 2000. "The Story of Urban Renewal." *Pittsburgh Post-Gazette,* May 21, 1, 2.

Foucault, Michel. 1971. *Archeology of Knowledge.* New York: Pantheon.

Franceschina, Angelo. 1987. Head of Fountain Square–Fletcher Place Investment Corporation, City of Indianapolis. Interview by author, May 23.

Freligh, B. 1998. "A New Surge of Pride on the South Side." *Cleveland Plain Dealer,* Feb. 22, sec. 1, 6.

Friedman, D. 1980. "Public Housing and the Poor." In *Housing Urban America,* edited by J. Pyness, R. Schafer, and C. W. Hartman, 473–84. New York: Aldine.

Gailey, Paul. 1986. "Nine Weeks, Ten Murders." *Chicago Sun-Times,* Mar. 22, 66.

Glazer, Nathan. 1970. *Cities in Trouble.* Quadrangle: Chicago.

Glickman, Norman. 1980. *The Urban Impacts of Federal Policies.* Baltimore: Johns Hopkins Univ. Press.

Goodrich, Peter. 1987. *Legal Discourse: Studies in Linguistics, Rhetoric, and Legal Analysis.* New York: St. Martin's.

Gow, Hann Bradford. 1993. "Lack of Morals Creates Violence." *Michigan Chronicle,* Mar. 3, A-6.

Greggs, LaTicia. 1992. "Gang-Lifestyle Gives Youths Peers, Support." *Chicago Defender,* Mar. 16, 1.

Hadjor, Kofi Buenor. 1997. *Another America: the Politics of Race and Blame.* Boston: South End.

Hampson, Rick. 1986. "Today's Ghetto Manchild Has No Promised Land." *San Francisco Chronicle,* Apr. 16, 18–23.

Harrington, Michael. 1962. *The Other America: Poverty in the United States.* New York: Macmillan.

Harris, Marcellus. 1991. "We Must All Work Together." *Atlanta Journal and Guide,* Feb. 5, 8.

Harris, S. 1994. "Fightin It Out." *Akron-Beacon Journal* 4 (June): 14.

Harvard Business Review. 1977. "Global Cities of Tomorrow." May–June, 79–92.

Harvey, David. 1981. "The Urban Process under Capitalism: A Framework for Analysis." In *Urbanization and Urban Planning in Capitalist Society,* edited by M. Dear and A. J. Scott, 91–122. London: Methuen.

———. 1989. *The Condition of Postmodernity.* Oxford, UK: Blackwell.

Heredia, Carlos. 1992. Director, Por Un Barrio Mejor, Chicago. Interview by author, Sept. 10.

Heritage Foundation. 1994. "Crime Rates and Welfare Spending." Available from Heritage Foundation, Washington, D.C.

———. 1998. "Issues 98: Chapter 11: Alternatives to Racial Preferences." Available from author.

Herman, Charles, Harold K. Jacobson, and Anne S. Moffat. 1997. *Violent Conflict in the Twenty-first Century: Causes, Instruments, and Mitigation.* Conference paper, American Academy of Arts and Sciences Conference, May, Chicago, Illinois.

Higginbotham, Evelyn Brooks. 1995. "The Feminist Theology of Black Baptist Church, 1880–1900." In *Religion and American Culture,* edited by D. G. Hackett, 16–28. New York: Routledge.

———. 1997. "The Black Church: A Gender Perspective." In *African American Religion,* edited by T. E. Fulop and A. J. Raboteau, 45–54. New York: Routledge.

Hill, Mike. 1997. *Whiteness: A Critical Reader.* New York: New York Univ. Press.

hooks, bell. 1992. 1993. *Outlaw Culture: Resisting Representations.* New York: Routledge.

House Democratic Policy Committee. 1996. "Downsizing the American Dream." Staff report of the House Democratic Policy Committee, available from committee, Washington, D.C.

Howard, Glen. 1987. Member of Indianapolis City-County Council. Discussion with author, Nov. 3.

Hughes, Gordon. 1998. *Understanding Crime Prevention.* Buckingham, UK: Open Univ.

Hulquist, Michael. 1981. Introduction to *The Dialogic Imagination,* by Mikhail Bakhtin, 15–33. Austin: Univ. of Texas Press.

Human Rights Watch. 2000. "Out of Sight: Super-Maximum Security Confinement in the United States." Available from Human Rights Watch, New York, New York.

Humphrey, Hubert. 1948. "What's Wrong with Our Cities?" *The American City* 63 (July): 12–13.

Humphrey, Imani. 1992. "It's Another Case of Chickens Coming Home to Roost—Violence Spawns Violence." *Michigan Chronicle,* May 20, A-5.

Jackson, Jim. 2001. "The Path to the Inner City." *Suppressed News,* Apr. 27, 4.

Jackson, Peter. 1988. "Street Life: The Politics of Carnival." *Society and Space* 6:213–27.

———. 1989. "Geography, Race, and Racism." In *New Models in Geography,* edited by R. Peet and N. Thrift. London: Unwin and Hyman.

Jacobs, Jane. 1961. *The Death and Life of Great American Cities.* New York: Vintage.

Jakle, John A., and David Wilson. 1992. *Derelict Landscapes: The Wasting of America's Built Environment.* Lanham, Md.: Rowman and Littlefield.

Jarrett, Vernon. 1974. "Self-Determination Must Be Regained." *Chicago Tribune,* Jan. 27, sec. 5, 1.

Jefferson, Nancy. 1991. Local politician, Chicago. Interview by author, Oct. 23.

Jonas, Andrew, and David Wilson. 1999. *The Urban Growth Machine: Critical Appraisals Two Decades Later.* Albany: State Univ. of New York Press.

Judd, Dennis R. 1979. *The Politics of American Cities: Private Power and Public Policy.* Glenview, Ill.: Little, Brown College Division.

Kaplan, Cora. 1996. "A Cavern Opened in My Mind: The Politics of Homosexuality and the Politics of Masculinity in James Baldwin." In *Representing Black Men,* edited by K. M. Blount and G. Cunningham, 43–58. London: Routledge.

Kaplan, Harold. 1966. "Urban Renewal in Newark." In *Urban Renewal: The Record and the Controversy,* edited by J. Q. Wilson, 233–58. Boston: MIT Press.

Keith, Michael. 1993. *Race, Riots, and Policing.* London: UCL.

Kelley, Robin D. G. 1997. *Yo' Mama's Disfunctional.* Boston: Beacon.

Kennedy, Liam. 2000. *Race and Urban Space in Contemporary American Culture.* Edinburgh, Scotland: Edinburgh Univ.

Kirby, David. 1999. "Stonewall Veterans Recall the Outlaw Days." *New York Times,* June 27, 3.

Kirschenbaum, Jill. 1995. "Code Enforcement Conundrum." *City Limits,* May, 19–20.

Knight, Cranston. 1994. "Thoughts on Black-on-Black Crime." *Chicago Defender,* Feb. 24, 12.

Knopp, Larry, and Richard Kujawa. 1993. "Ideology and Urban Landscapes: Conceptions of the Market in Portland, Maine." *Antipode* 25:114–39.

Kotulak, Ronald. 1990. "Study Finds Inner-City Kids Live with Violence." *Chicago Tribune,* Sept. 28, sec. 1, 5.

LaBaj, John. 1986. Manager, Division of Economic and Housing Development, Department of Metropolitan Development, City of Indianapolis. Discussion with author, May 14.

Laws, Glenda. 1997. "Globalization, Immigration, and Changing Social Relations in U.S. Cities." *Annals of the American Academy of Social and Political Science* 551:89–104.

Lee, Felicia. 1989. "East New York, Haunted by Crime, Fights for Its Life." *New York Times,* Jan. 5, sec. 2, 2.

———. 1996. "The Black Underclass: Living in a Violent, Dispirited World." *New York Times,* Oct. 3, 17.

Lefebvre, Henri. 1984. *The Production of Space.* Oxford, UK: Blackwell.

Lemke, Jay. 1995. *Textual Politics: Discourse and Social Dynamics.* London: Taylor and Francis.

Levitan, Sar A. 1985. *Programs in Aid of the Poor.* Baltimore: Johns Hopkins Univ. Press.

Limbaugh, Rush. 1992. Commentary on the *Rush Limbaugh Show,* nationally syndicated talk presentation. Dec., WDWS, Champaign, Illinois.

———. 1995. Commentary on the *Rush Limbaugh Show,* nationally syndicated talk presentation. Oct., WDWS, Champaign, Illinois.

Lincoln, Bruce. 1989. *Discourse and the Construction of Society.* New York: Oxford Univ. Press.

Lineberry, Robert L., and Ira Sharkansky. 1978. *Urban Politics and Public Policy.* New York: Harper and Row.

Long, Norton. 1971. "The City as Reservation." *The Public Interest* 25 (Fall): 30–38.

Los Angeles Sentinel. 1985. "Let's Clean It Up." *Los Angeles Sentinel,* Nov. 14, A-6.

———. 1986. "Crisis Equals Epidemic." *Los Angeles Sentinel,* Feb. 27, A-6.

———. 1989a. "Editorial: A Touch of Irony." *Los Angeles Sentinel,* Mar. 30, A-6.

Lott, Tommy. 1999. *The Invention of Race.* Oxford, UK: Blackwell.

Loury, Glenn C. 1985. "The Moral Quandary of the Black Community." *The Public Interest* 79 (Spring): 9–23.

Lucas, Don. 1991. Planner, City of Chicago. Discussion with author, Aug. 10.

Lusane, Clarence. 1993. "Rhapsodic Aspirations: Rap, Race, and Power Politics." *Black Scholar* 23:37–51.

Lyotard, Jean François. 1984. *The Postmodern Condition.* Minneapolis: Univ. of Minnesota Press.

Males, Mike. 1997. *The Scapegoat Generation: America's War on Adolescents.* Monroe, Maine: Common Courage.

———. 1999. *Framing Youth: Ten Myths about the Next Generation.* Monroe, Maine: Common Courage.

Males, Mike, and Dan Macalair. 1999. "The Effects of Three Strikes Laws on Crime in California." *Stanford Review of Law and Policy,* Fall, 169–78.

Mallory, Rik. 1991. Local politician, City of St. Louis. Discussion with author, July 11.

Malveaux, Julianne. 1993. "Crisis or Power Struggle? The Future of Urban Areas." *Black Scholar* 23:11–15.

Marable, Manning. 1995. "History and Black Consciousness: The Political Culture of Black America." *Monthly Review* 47 (July–Aug.): 71–88.

Marino, Bruce, Vincent J. Roscigno, and Patricia L. McCall. 1998. "Structure, Agency, and Context in the Reproduction of Black-on-Black Violence." *Theoretical Criminology* 2:29–55.

Martinez, Glenn. 1994. "Gangs Trouble Sonoma County." *San Francisco Chronicle,* Feb. 22, A-1.

Marx, Karl. 1970. *Eighteenth Brumaire.* Ann Arbor: Univ. of Michigan Press.

Maxwell, Christopher, and Timothy Bynum. 1999. "Michigan's Sentencing and Incarceration in the Context of Rising and Falling Crime Rates." East Lansing, Mich.: Institute for Public Policy and Social Research.

McCarthy, Cameron. 1995. "Danger in the Safety Zone: Notes on Race, Resentment, and the Discourse of Crime, Violence, and Suburban Security." Univ. of Illinois Dept. of Educational Policy Studies, Champaign-Urbana, Illinois, unpublished manuscript.

McClain, Leonita. 1982. "Give the Angels a Chance." *Chicago Tribune,* May 12, A-6.

McCollum, Dan. 1995. Mayor of Champaign, Illinois. Interview by author, Oct. 29.

Mercer, Kobena. 1997. *Welcome to the Jungle: New Positions in Black Cultural Studies.* London: Routledge.

Merridew, Alan. 1975a. "Profile of Crime in Chicago Shows It's Skyrocketing in White Districts." *Chicago Tribune,* Sept. 11, sec. 1, 1.

Miller, Lorraine. 1989. "Mama Makes Difference—Even in Court." *New York Amsterdam News,* Saturday, Aug. 5, 7.

Miller, Walter B. 1958. "Lower Class Culture as a Generating Milieu of Gang Delinquency." *Journal of Social Issues* 14:5–19.

Moldthan, Carl. 1987. Candidate for mayor of Indy Pendence Party, Indianapolis. Discussion with author, May 26.

Montgomery, Robert. 1966. "Improving the Design in Urban Renewal." In *Urban Renewal: The Record and the Controversy,* edited by J. Q. Wilson, 454–87. Boston: MIT Press.

Morial, Marc. 2000. "Press Release: Survey on Gun Deaths." Website www .nul.org/documents/Marcskeyunote.doc/.

Moynihan, Daniel. 1965. "The Negro Family: The Case for National Action." Technical report, U.S. Department of Labor, Office of Policy Planning and Research, Washington, D.C.

———. 1966. "Is There Really an Urban Crisis?" *Challenge* 15 (Nov./Dec.).

Muller, Peter O. 1981. *Contemporary Suburban America.* Englewood Cliffs, N.J.: Prentice-Hall.

———. 2000. Professor of geography, Univ. of Miami. Personal correspondence, May 18.

Mumby, Dennis K. 1993. "Introduction: Narrative and Social Control." In *Narrative and Social Control: Critical Perspectives,* edited by Dennis K. Mumby, 1–15. Newbury Park, Calif.: Sage.

Municipal Research Services Center. 1997. "Juvenile Curfews." Unpublished document, available from Univ. of Washington

Murray, Charles. 1984. *Losing Ground: American Social Policy, 1950–1980.* New York: Basic Books.

Nadell, James. 1995. "Boys N the Hood: A Colonial Discourse." *Journal of Black Studies* 25 (Mar.): 447–64.

National Center for Policy Analysis. 1997. "Ten Facts on Crime." Technical report. Dallas, Texas.

———. 1998. "Crime and Punishment in America." Technical document. Dallas, Texas.

National Committee for Responsive Philanthropy. 1997. "Moving a Public Policy Agenda: The Strategic Philanthropy of Conservative Foundations." Washington, D.C.: NCRP.

National Institute of Corrections. 1999. "Supermax Prisons: Overview and General Considerations." Washington, D.C.: U.S. Department of Justice.

National Journal of Sexual Orientation. 1993. "Coming Out and Stepping Up: Queer Legal Theory and Connectivity." *National Journal of Sexual Orientation* 1:3–43.

New York Times. 1953. "Federal Aided Project, Public Project and Higher-Rent Planned." *New York Times,* Aug. 24, 4.

———. 1994. "Prominent Blacks Stress Family, Church, and School as Instruments to Fight Violence." *New York Times,* Jan. 1, 16.

Nixon, Richard. 1969. Presidential address in State of the Union Speech, unpublished document, Richard Nixon Library, Yorba Linda, California.

Nolan, J. 1993. "Geographies of Learning: Theatre Studies, Performance, and the Performative." *Theatre Journal* 45:417–44.

Norman, Michael. 1993. "One Cop, Eight Square Blocks." *New York Times Magazine,* Dec. 12, 62–71.

Norton, Anne. 1993. *Republic of Signs.* Chicago: Univ. of Chicago Press.

Oliver, Pamela. 2000. "Racial Disparities on Imprisonment." Paper presented at Prison Awareness Week, Oct. 22–28, Madison, Wisconsin.

Oliver, William. 1989. "Sexual Conquest and Patterns of Black-on-Black Violence." Abstract, *Sociological Abstracts.*

Osofsky, Gilbert. 1966. *Harlem: The Making of a Ghetto.* New York: Harper and Row.

Packard, Vance. 1960. *The Waste Makers.* New York: David McKay.

Page, Clarence. 1984. "Jackson Is Running Against Crime, and Why Not for Mayor?" *Chicago Tribune,* Oct. 16, 2.

———. 1987. "An Emotionally Loaded Political Weapon." *Chicago Tribune,* Jan. 14, sec. 1, 2.

———. 1988. "Sorting Out America's Racial Puzzle." *Chicago Tribune,* Jan. 3, 3.

Palen, Michael. 1995. *The Suburbs.* New York: McGraw Hill.

Parenti, Bart. 1984. Indianapolis councilman. Discussion with author, June 9.

Parisi, Peter, and Briavel Holcomb. 1994. "Symbolizing Place: Journalistic Narratives of the City." *Urban Geography* 15:376–94.

Parsons, Monique. 1999. "Pulpits Step in When System Fails." *Home News Tribune,* Jan. 11, 6.

Perkins, Usani. 1991. *The Ghettcolony.* Chicago: Univ. of Chicago Press.

Pierson, Harry D. 1993. "Stigma of Violence and Youths." *Chicago Defender,* Oct. 20, A-7.

Pinckney, Alphonso. 1990. *The Myth of Black Progress.* Cambridge, UK: Cambridge Univ. Press.

Plann, Joe. 2000. Planner, City of St. Louis. Interview with author, Oct. 26.

Potter, Jonathan. 1996. *Representing Reality: Discourse, Rhetoric, Social Construction.* Thousand Oaks, Calif.: Sage.

Pred, Allen. 1984. "Place as Historically Contingent Process: Structuration and the Time Geography of Becoming Places." *Annals of the Association of American Geographers* 74:279–97.

Presdee, Mike. 2000. *Cultural Criminology and the Carnival of Crime.* London: Routledge.

Pulido, Laura. 1998. "A Critical Review of the Methodology of Environmental Racism Research." *Antipode* 28:142–59.

Rafsky, William. 1978. Urban Renewal Director, City of Philadelphia. Presentation and discussion before graduate policy class, Temple Univ., Feb. 12.

Rainwater, Lee. 1966. "Crucible of Identity: The Lower Class Negro Family." *Daedalus* 45:172–96.

Raymond, Eric. 1990. "Whatever Became of Civil Rights?" *Philadelphia Inquirer,* Feb. 8.

Reagan, Ronald. 1981. First Inaugural Address, State of the Union Speech, Jan. 20, Washington, D.C. Ronald Reagan Presidential Library, Simi Valley, California.

———. 1982. State of the Union Speech, Jan. 19, Washington, D.C. Ronald Reagan Presidential Library, Simi Valley, California.

Reynolds, Morgan O. 1998. "Weeping for the Criminal?" Technical report, Heartland Institute, Chicago, Illinois, June/July.

Rhodes, Stu. 1986. City-county councilor, City of Indianapolis. Interview by author, June 11.

Romney, George. 1972. In *U.S. News and World Report* 72 (Apr. 10): 40–46.

Rossi, Rosalind. 1981. "Lawmen Focus on Combating Use of Juveniles in Gang Crime." *Chicago Sun-Times,* May 3, 50.

Ruddick, Sue. 1996a. *Young and Homeless in Hollywood: Mapping Social Identities.* New York: Routledge.

———. 1996b. "Constructing Difference in Public Spaces: Race, Class, and Gender as Interlocking System." *Urban Geography* 17:132–51.

St. Louis Home Project. 1999. Presentation on City of St. Louis, website http://stlouis.Missouri.org/.

Salins, Peter. 1980. *The Ecology of Housing Destruction.* New York: Doubleday.

Schanberg, Sydney H. 1985. "A Lot of Talk about Crime." *New York Times,* Mar. 19, 25.

Schein, Richard. 1999. "Teaching 'Race' and the Cultural Landscape." *Journal of Geography* 98:188–90.

Scheingold, Stuart A. 1991. *The Politics of Street Crime.* Philadelphia: Temple Univ. Press.

Schiraldi, Vincent. 1998. "How Distorted Coverage of Juvenile Crime Affects Public Policy." Technical report. Justice Policy Institute, Washington, D.C.

Schlosser, Eric. 1998. "The Prison–Industrial Complex." *Atlantic Monthly,* Dec., 40–48.

Schneider, Dorothea. 1988. " 'I Know All about Emma Lazarus': Nationalism and Its Contradictions in Congressional Rhetoric of Immigration Restrictions." *Cultural Anthropology* 13:82–99.

Schneider, Rob. 1987. Writer for *Indianapolis Star.* Interview by author, June 4.

Shields, Rob. 1991. *Places on the Margin: Alternative Geographies of Modernity*. London: Routledge.

———. 1997. "Spatial Stress and Resistance: Social Meanings of Specialization." In *Space and Social Theory*, edited by George Binko and Ulf Strohmayer, 186–202. Oxford, UK: Blackwell.

Short, John Rennie. 1996. *The Urban Order*. Oxford, UK: Blackwell.

———. 1999. "Urban Imagineers: Boosterism and the Representation of Cities." In *The Urban. Growth Machine: Critical Perspectives Two Decades Later*, edited by A.E.G. Jones and D. Wilson, 37–54. Albany: State Univ. of New York Press.

Silverman, Charles E. 1994. "Truth and Justice." *New York Times*, Jan. 30, sec. 4, 1.

Simon, Roger. 1981. "Law of Jungle Etched in Concrete." *Chicago Sun-Times*, Oct. 1, 7.

Smith, Neil. 1996. *The New Urban Frontier: Gentrification and the Revanchist City*. Oxford, UK: Blackwell.

Smith, Neil, and Peter Williams. 1986. *Gentrification and the City*. London: Allen and Unwin.

Smith, William French. 1991. *Law and Justice in the Reagan Administration: The Memoirs of an Attorney General*. Stanford, Calif.: Hoover Institute.

Socialism Today. 1999. "The Stonewall Riots, 1969." *Socialism Today* 40 (July/Aug.): 24–28.

Solomon, Arthur. 1974. *Housing the Urban Poor: A Critical Evaluation of Federal Housing Policy*. Cambridge, Mass: MIT Press.

Soja, Edward. 1989. *Postmodern Geographers*. London: Verso.

———. 1996. *Third Space*. London: Verso.

Soll, Rick. 1985. "Sucker: Gang Stoolie's Deadly Life." *Chicago Sun-Times*, Mar. 29, 7.

Sowell, Thomas. 1984. *Civil Rights: Rhetoric or Reality?* New York: William Morrow.

———. 1985. *The Economics and Politics of Race*. New York: William Morrow and Co.

———. 1988. "Courtroom's the Battle in Our Continuing Cultural Wars." *Champaign-Urbana News Gazette* Sept. 6, 7.

———. 2001. "Life at the Bottom." *Jewish World Review*, Nov. 1, 4.

Stallybrass, Peter, and Allan White. 1986. *The Politics and Parties of Transgression*. Ithaca, N.Y.: Cornell Univ. Press.

Steinfels, Peter. 1979. *The Neoconservatives*. New York: Simon and Schuster.

Steny, Mark. 1999. "Photo Co-Opt." *National Review,* Mar. 31, 12.

Sternlieb, George. 1966. *The Tenement Landlord.* New Brunswick, N.J.: CUPR.

————. 1970. *The Tenement Landlord Revisited.* New Brunswick, N.J.: CUPR.

Still, Bayrd. 1974. *Urban America.* Boston: Little, Brown and Co.

Stolinsky, David. 2000. "America: The Most Violent Nation?" *Medical Sentinel* 6, 199–201.

Streib, Victor. 2000. "The Juvenile Death Penalty Today: Death Sentences and Executions for Juvenile Crimes." Website, www.ncpc.org/ncpc/pg=2088-6546/.

Taylor, Jon Marc. 1996. "The Great Dumbbell Theft." *Prison News Service,* Spring, 1–3.

Teaford, Jon. 1990. *The Rough Road to Renaissance.* Baltimore: Johns Hopkins Univ. Press.

Teague, George. 1998. "Commonly Asked Questions and Answers about New York City's Lesbian and Gay Pride Day." Unpublished manuscript.

Thomas, Lee. 1991. Planner, City of Chicago. Discussion with author, Aug. 18.

Time Almanac. 1990. Chicago, Ill.: *Time* Publishers.

Tonry, Michael, and Norvel Morris. 1984. *Crime and Justice.* Chicago: Univ. of Chicago Press.

Turnout. 1998. Website dedicated to gay and lesbian politics, www.turnout.org/.

University Village Association. 1991. Head of association. Discussion with author, Mar. 4.

U.S. Census Bureau. 1980a. "Characteristics of the Population Below the Poverty Level, 1978." *Current Population Reports.* Series P-60. Washington, D.C.: U.S. Government Printing Office.

————. 1980b. "Social, Economic, and Housing Characteristics of the Population." Washington, D.C.: U.S. Department of Commerce.

U.S. Conference of Mayors. 1997. "Press Release 347—City Survey on Youth Curfews." Washington, D.C.: U.S. Conference of Mayors.

U.S. News and World Report. 1967a. "Anarchy Growing Threat to Big Cities." *U.S. News and World Report* 63 (Aug. 7): 28.

————. 1967b. "Not All This Country Is Tense, Troubled." *U.S. News and World Report* 63 (Aug. 7): 37.

————. 1972a. "Vast Cities Breaking Down into a Jungle." *U.S. News and World Report,* Apr. 10, 46.

————. 1972b. "After Billions to Rescue Cities." *U.S. News and World Report* 72, Apr. 10.

———. 1975. "Any Way You Look at It: The Worst Slump Since the 1930s." *U.S. News and World Report,* Mar. 31, 26–31.

———. 1986. "The Black Underclass." *U.S. News and World Report,* Apr. 14, 78.

Van Allsberg, Mark. 1975. "Property Abandonment in Detroit." *Wayne Law Review* 20:25–37.

Village Voice. 1999. "The Supermax Solution." *Village Voice,* May 11–17, 19.

Vieth, John A. 1990. "Evangelizing Our Inner Circle." Unpublished technical document.

Von Hoffman, Nicholas. 1981. "The Real Terror Is in the Streets." *Chicago Tribune,* Mar. 14, 9.

Wacquant, Loic. 1994a. "The Ghetto, the State, and the New Capitalist Economy." In *Metropolis,* edited by Phil Kascintz, 508–18. New York: New York Univ. Press.

———. 1994b. "Dangerous Places: Violence and Isolation in Chicago's Black Belt and the Parisian Red Belt." Mimeo from author.

Wagner-Pacifici, Robin. 1994. *Discourse and Social Destruction.* Chicago: Univ. of Chicago Press.

Waldrep, Heather. 1995. "The New Superpredator." *Southern Nazarene,* available from author.

Walker, Richard. 1981. "A Theory of Suburbanization: Capitalism and the Construction of Urban Space in the United States." In *Urbanization and Planning in Capitalist Society,* edited by M. Dear and A. J. Scott, 339–82. London: Methuen.

Walkowitz, Judith. 1992. *City of Dreadful Delight.* Chicago: Univ. of Chicago Press.

Weaver, Robert C. 1966. *The Urban Complex.* New York: Doubleday.

Weicher, John. 1970. *Urban Renewal.* Washington: Urban Land Institute.

Weiler, Michael, and W. Barnett Pearce. 1992a. *Reagan and Public Discourse in America.* Tuscaloosa: Univ. of Alabama Press.

———. 1992b. "Ceremonial Discourse: The Rhetorical Ecology of the Reagan Administration." In *Reagan and Public Discourse in America,* edited by Michael Weiler and W. Barnett Pearce, 11–42. Tuscaloosa: Univ. of Alabama Press.

Weingarten, Paul. 1982. "Mean Streets: In This West Side Story, the Violence Is Very Real." *Chicago Tribune,* Sept. 9, 1.

West, Ben. 1987. City-county councilor, City of Indianapolis. Interview by author, Oct. 14.

White, Evelyn C., and Thaii Walker. 1994. "Violence Is Poignant Pain for Blacks." *San Francisco Chronicle,* Dec. 23, 10–18.

White, John. 1980. "Fighting the Odds." *Chicago Tribune,* Oct. 21, 16–19.

Wilayto, Phil. 2000. "Wisconsin's Exploding Prison Population: The Bradley Connection." Paper presented at Prison Awareness Week, Oct. 22-28, Madison, Wisconsin.

Wilkerson, Isabel. 1989. "Separate and Unequal: A View from Above." *New York Times,* Mar. 1, A-12.

Williams, Walter. 1985. "Why Do We Pay the Price?" *Chicago Tribune,* Jan. 12, 12.

Wilson, David. 1996. "Metaphors, Growth Coalition Discourses and Black Poverty Neighborhoods." *Antipode* 28:72–96.

———. 2001. "Colouring the City: 'Black-on-Black Violence' and Liberal Discourse." *Tidschrift Voor Economische En Sociale Geografie* 92:261–78.

Wilson, David, and Dennis Grammenos. 2000. "Spatiality and Urban Redevelopment Movements." *Urban Geography* 21:361–71.

Wilson, James Q. 1966. *Urban Renewal: The Record and the Controversy.* Cambridge, Mass: MIT Press.

———. 1970. "Why We Are Having a Wave of Violence." In *Cities in Trouble,* edited by N. Glazer, 55–66. Chicago: Quandrangle.

Wilson, William Julius. 1987. *The Truly Disadvantaged.* Chicago: Univ. of Chicago Press.

Wright, Elizabeth. 1988. "Needed: A Moral Revival." *Cleveland Call & Post,* Dec. 22, B-9.

Yin, Robert. 1994. *Qualitative Methods.* Newbury Park, Calif.: Sage.

Youthspeak. 2000. "Youth Curfews." Technical document, www.youthspeak @oblivion.net.

Ziff, Ellen. 1981. "Fighting New Crime." *Chicago Tribune,* Feb. 8, 2.

Zoglin, R. 1996. "Now for the Bad News: A Teenage Time Bomb." *Time,* Jan. 15, 51–53.

Zuckerman, Mortimer B. 1986. "Black America's Mirror Image." *U.S. News and World Report,* May 6, 17.

Index

Page number in italic type denotes a table or chart.